Workplace Jerks! Will This Person be a Speed Bump, a Pothole or a Landmine? has sold more than two dozen copies worldwide to date. If you buy a copy and you actually read it, then I don't think you're a jerk.

In this book I describe people who are not like you. You know, pain in the asses, or pains in the ass, or possibly pains in the asses - - whatever. You know, jerks.

Well, jerks are everywhere and they are particularly bad at work. After all, most of us have to work and we can't get away from them. Here, not only do I describe workplace jerks but I suggest ways to avoid hiring them and ways cope with them if you already have them.

Make the purchase and I'll bet that you'll save more on aspirin than the cost of this book.

Workplace Jerks!

Will This Person be a Speed Bump, a Pothole or a Landmine?

Dale G. Paulson, Ph.D.

CreateSpace.com

Dedication

Book dedications are strange things. They force you to think about people who are important to you so you can thank them but then, in the process of writing the dedication, one is reminded that you probably should have thanked them already. I should have been more diligent because these are very special people.

Therefore I dedicate this book to four very special people.

To **David Steinberg**, a gentleman who has moved from octogenarian to nonagenarian and who is a good friend. He has done many interesting things, not the least of which includes helping to draft the Marshall Plan. I'm glad that he did because it is one of the many things that makes me proud to be an American.

To **Tom Gorski**, the nicest man I know. He is an association executive and C.E.O. and was always supportive and encouraging of my research, but I think he prefers the title "Family Man." He is also a very talented cartoonist who drew the turkey cartoon found in this book.

To **George Mohr**, a dear friend of many years. I see him seldom now because we live on opposite sides of the country but we still find time to laugh together. George suffered a heart attack about twenty years ago and during that episode a nurse leaned over to assist. The top button of her dress was unbuttoned and with what could have been his final words George muttered, "Nice tits." How can you not like someone like that? Since that experience, George has created flying snakes, spiritual shields, and photographs that hint at divine intervention.

To my wife **Leah**, I know that I've told you how important you are to me - - but probably not enough. We share float plans, business plans, and creative plans and sometimes all at once.

Also by Dale Paulson

Allegiance®: Fulfilling the Promise of One-to-One Marketing for Associations

Table of Contents

FOREWORD

By Dave Caperton, author of ***Happiness Is a Funny Thing***

I believe that fun is serious business. Put another way, I believe that businesses that are serious about success should actively make enjoyment a part of the work experience. Wouldn't you agree that individuals who enjoy what they do tend to be better at it than those who don't? Probably, you do. Would it surprise you to learn that organizations with happy workers generally enjoy higher profitability and productivity, lower absenteeism, fewer accidents and lawsuits than those organizations with morale issues? Probably it wouldn't. Enjoyment enhances the quality of the outcomes primarily because it improves the quality of the input. When I enjoy doing something, I want to do it well.

The value of joy is not really debatable but how to reliably create it is. My job as a speaker and writer on the value of joy and happiness is to provide steps that lead to greater joy and a better chance of individual and organizational success. What I've learned over the years is that happiness at work and at home is about many things, but probably none is so important as the quality of interpersonal relationships. Over the years that I've traveled around the country spreading the gospel of joyfulness, I've seen organizations that are healthy and energized, and I've worked with more than a few that were struggling with low morale, poor customer service and were riddled with internal conflict. In these cases where the work environment was toxic, the story was predictably and depressingly similar: there were a handful of bad apple employees (or maybe just one or two toxic bosses) who had hijacked the entire organization and poisoned the work environment. The result was a place where the focus had been pulled away from the mission or the needs of the customers and was instead concentrated upon conflict and manufactured drama that seem to be the only thing that judgmental, entitled, vindictive, adversarial, undisciplined personalities can reliably produce. If such experiences and poisonous personalities were rarities in the workplace we might just learn how to ignore them, but they seem to be everywhere.

Ben Franklin once said "In this world nothing can be certain except death and taxes." If you ask Dale Paulson, he would probably add "and jerks" to that short list. Everyone has to endure the occasional jerk. It's the guy who stares straight ahead to keep from making eye contact as he refuses to let anyone ahead of his car on the way out of a crowded parking lot. It's the woman who texts during a dinner conversation making it clear that a virtual conversation with a person who is not there is overwhelmingly preferable to a real conversation with you. It's the weasel who takes credit for your work at the office, the teen who talks all through the movie you just paid $10 to see, the cynic, the know-it-all, the bully, the zealot and the negaholic who traps you in the break room for the latest installment of his or her on-going whine-a-thon.

The prevalence of jerks in the workplace begs the question, "So how did these horrible people get a job in the first place?" Because getting a job and doing a job require two completely different skill sets, some jerks are actually quite good at interviewing and getting hired only to shed their good-guy disguises later. But what if we could do the job applicant equivalent of an airport x-ray and see beneath personable façade and the rehearsed answers to standard interview questions? That's what Dale Paulson's Allegiance Research assessment tool called the Workplace Attitudes Test (WAT) was designed to do. Using this instrument that he developed, employers now have a fighting chance of avoiding hiring jerks and paying the high price of the ensuing damage that they can cause.

I have to admit that I was surprised by Paulson's research that about 5% of respondents of the WAT scored highly enough on the 9 jerk categories to be considered a risk of being what he calls "a speed bump, a pothole, or a landmine." That's one out of every twenty people! That still may seem like a lower number than you expected (frankly, I assumed the number would at least be as high as the percentage of people who didn't vote as I did in the last election). Still, one out of twenty is pretty sobering. Think about nineteen other people you know. Are any of them jerks? If you said

Yes, then you can see how prevalent the problem of jerks is in your life (of course, if none of those nineteen people you thought of are jerks, then it must be you).

Employers who want to hire smarter will find the insights in this book some of the most valuable anywhere. The people you hire will create innovative solutions or unnecessary problems. They will delight or alienate your customers. They will unite or divide your team. They will enhance or detract from your brand. The best time to find out the value or cost that they're likely to represent is before they're on the payroll. A jerk-free environment is a place to work and innovate, to serve and succeed. Frankly it's a place to profit and have fun together and that's not a trivial thing because, as I've said before, fun is serious business.

Dave Caperton,
Speaker, educator
and author of
Happiness Is a Funny Thing
(Alcus Media, 2009)
www.davecaperton.com
740-JOY-FULY

"Just because Ben Franklin
wanted to make the turkey the national bird
doesn't mean you have to hire one!"

Introduction

**Jerks Are Everywhere -- Don't be One,
Don't Hire One, But Learn How to
Cope With One**

This book explains a lot about jerk behavior. Jerks are everywhere. You will find them at churches or temples, at workplaces, at social gatherings, at sporting events, at restaurants, and you probably encountered a few while driving. If you are brave enough to ride a bike, then you really know about jerks. Heck, you can even see them on television or listen to them on the radio, and I'm not just talking about "America's Most Wanted."

In a sense, jerks are "America's Least Wanted" and you need some strategies to cope with them. Jerks cause problems everywhere but it can be worse in the workplace. Why? Because in the workplace they are hard to avoid and you probably have to interact with them. They can also be abusive to clients and customers who are the cornerstone of any enterprise. While you can walk away from an abusive person at a social gathering or move away from an abusive driver, most of us simply cannot walk away from a job.

For the purposes of this book, a jerk is someone who is disruptive in the workplace. They can be rude and difficult to work with. Jerks at work cause tremendous stress, they cost money, and sometimes the boss is the last to know. As a person who studies human behavior and designs research instruments, I decided to step up to the plate and take a look at workplace jerks. As a result, I identified *nine attitudes* that should be measured before hiring, and a related pre-employment test called the *Workplace Attitudes Test*™. This test is different, even revolutionary, because unlike traditional hiring practices **it looks for the bad, not the good**. The bottom line: it measures nine work-related attitudes and identifies possible warning signals.

1

Are You the Ideal Customer for This Book?

This book is for anyone who encounters jerks, particularly at work. This includes employees, employers, HR consultants, and polite people who need strategies to cope with jerks at work and elsewhere. Maybe you have to work with a jerk and would like to know more about how to deal with them. In that case, this book provides you with some coping strategies. If you are a person who hires and promotes, and would like a new tool, this book describes nine attitudes that can be warning signals and how we test for them. And for all of you out there, this book has some stories both light and serious that provide a little enlightenment.

Is This You?

Maybe you are in a position to decide or influence who gets hired or promoted. If so, is your story?

"I sometimes hire the wrong people. This opens me up to potential lawsuits, lost merchandise, lost customers and unhappy employees. When I promote the wrong person, the results are more disastrous. I thought that I was a good interviewer and I do background checks but bad employees are still hired and/or promoted."

Or maybe, this is your story?

"Traditional pre-employment tests don't always work well and HR professionals at my company don't help much because they seem to be more afraid of making a mistake than I am. In job interviews everyone is on their best behavior and the interviewer does not say rude things like 'You seem very judgmental' or 'You seem very vindictive.' I don't have time for this but I can't keep making the same mistakes. I often hire a jerk."

Or maybe you have a co-worker like one of these?

"My co-worker uses perfume even though I told her I am allergic and get headaches."

"My co-worker is prejudiced and talks about groups in negative ways even though I asked him to stop."

"My co-worker does little work during regular hours so he can do most of the work after hours and get paid time-and-a-half. This makes it very hard for us to work together and meet some deadlines."

How Can This Help?

Look, what you need is to avoid disruptive employees in your workplace. The best way to do this is to identify potential employees who have the attitudes that you *don't* want. Unfortunately, the job interview does not do a good job at identifying bad attitudes because people will say what they think you want to hear, and most pre-employment tests concentrate on *desirable* characteristics. My solution works because it is like an upside down cake -- the only purpose is to identify job applicants who may have *bad* attitudes.

If you test for good workplace attitudes, you will always find some good attitudes. Everyone has some good attitudes, but not everyone has bad attitudes. Look for what you **don't** want -- the bad attitudes -- otherwise you will miss them.

I am reminded of the lecture by an engineer who worked for a gold-mining operation. He said, "One has to sift through two tons of dirt to find one once of gold." Someone from the audience asked, "Wow, how is that possible?" and he replied, "You look for the gold not the dirt."

In somewhat of an irony, I believe that you must test for *good* behavior by looking for *bad* attitudes. As one of my clients said, "We hire good employees by not hiring bad ones."

If you already have an employee, boss, or co-worker who is a jerk, then there are some coping strategies available to you. These range from knowing about laws that protect you in extreme cases such as sexual harassment, or prejudice that keeps you from being promoted, to understanding the games people play every day. While this book does not discuss specific laws, it does explain various types of jerk behavior and why people act this way, and it provides some references for those who want more information.

I made the assumption that the workplace is almost always a social environment and I wanted to understand individuals who do not get along well with others. This lead to my identifying the nine attitudes that can destroy a workplace.

Being a Jerk Once in a While
Doesn't Make You a Jerk

My workplace research was designed to identify enduring jerks, not people having a bad day or those with lesser people-skills.

This is similar to the distinction between "states" and "traits" described by Dr. Robert Sutton, Professor of Management at the Stanford School of Engineering. In his 2007 book, *The No Asshole Rule*, he notes that psychologists find that "states" are fleeting feelings, thoughts, and actions whereas "traits" are enduring personality characteristics.

States are often related to circumstances, while traits are related to beliefs and attitudes. It is generally accepted by social scientists that certain beliefs and attitudes are consistent with the behavior of jerks in the workplace.

In short, jerks act the way they do because they have certain beliefs and attitudes that determine their behavior. They tend to see the world in a way that justifies their actions.

We all have subjective lenses (beliefs and attitudes) through which we see our world. As Bertrand Russell, the British author, mathematician and philosopher, said, "There is not one world, but as many worlds as there are people in it."

My research shows that jerks see their world as a place of hostility, a place of winners and losers, and a place where courtesy and consideration have little value. Jerks are often able to "play-act" their way through a job interview but once they have the job, their negative beliefs and attitudes usually direct their behavior.

Fortunately, some pre-employment tests can provide us a lens to see how jerks view their world. Everyone can be a jerk once in a while. Being an occasional jerk doesn't mean that you are really a jerk.

If you are going to score high on a jerk test you are going to have to have strong opinions, harsh beliefs, and you have to act upon them. It's not enough to react badly when your toast is burned and things go downhill from there.

Is This Jerk a Speed Bump, a Pothole or a Landmine?

For a speed bump you have to slow down, for a pothole you may have to get your wheels realigned, but with a landmine you're lucky if you survive. Many people believe that hiring the wrong employee is like a speed bump but the more I read and listen, the more I believe that bad hires are more serious than that and can be potholes or landmines. Yes, I too hired a few jerks along the way and these experiences also helped me when identifying the attitudes and developing the test.

A **speed bump** is where you hire someone, put them on probation, and get rid of them after a week or so. They may have missed work without calling, came in late, or been rude to customers but you caught it early and the rest of the staff, or you, picked up the slack and not too much damage was done.

A **pothole** is where the morale of fellow workers is affected, some customers are lost, and it may be difficult to get rid of that employee. I will provide some real-life examples later in this book including when I hired a drama queen, a man on a power trip, and when I gave a second chance to a person who had been convicted of embezzlement in a previous job.

A **landmine** is best described by Lester Rosen who is a noted lawyer, lecturer and writer in the HR field. His article is entitled "Recruiting Russian Roulette: Why Every Placement Has the Potential to Put You Out of Business." It is at www.esrchek.com/wordpress (originally published on www.HR.Toolbox.com/blog). He writes, "It's a sobering thought, but every time a recruiting professional makes a placement, there is the possibility that a new hire can put him out of business."

According to Mr. Rosen, "Industry statistics suggest that up to 10% of applicants can have criminal records. Fraudulent misrepresentations as to education and employment occur in as much as 40% of the time according to some studies."

He points out that professionals in the staffing field are particularly vulnerable to "Negligent Hiring" lawsuits and goes on to say, "A staffing professional would need to show whether credentials and education were verified, whether past employment was checked, and whether a criminal background check was done."

I couldn't agree more but, in fact, everyone who is involved in hiring is vulnerable. Even if the dangers are only a speed bump, careful hiring is important. A good pre-employment test such as the one described in this book is only a part of the puzzle. It does not replace a good interview or a good background check. It does, however, provide a tool that focuses on the identification of bad attitudes and it helps identify some applicants that you may want to eliminate early. In other instances, such as some described in this book, you can identify an insidious jerk.

How to Hire a Really Bad Employee!

If you wanted, for some unknown reason, to hire the worst possible employee how would you proceed? I'm talking the worst, the absolute worst. The type of person with their own agenda, impossible to supervise, petty, quick to take offense, and on their best days hinting that they have a great lawyer.

But how do you know that you've found a really bad employee? Much like jury consultants who ask prospective jurors about their attitudes related to our legal system, you should ask prospective employees about their work-related attitudes.

Some problematic work-related attitudes include the following: an over-developed sense of importance; a sense that they are special; and a belief that they don't have to do anything extra because they are already there. We see this in the former beauty queen who refuses to give up her tiara. It's called deservedness or a sense of entitlement.

As we continue our search for the bad employee, we look for a lack of empathy which is the inability or disinclination to see things from the other person's perspective. Rhett Butler's famous comment, "Frankly my dear, I don't give a damn" is humorous in movies but not so good on the job. "Do you have this in a size five?" "Frankly, my dear . . ."

We also need some pettiness and a good memory for remembering slights. If you can't hold a grudge, you don't qualify here. "Tower, this is Aardvark 551, requesting permission to proceed to Runway one eight." "Aardvark 551, do you remember what you said to me the last time you were at this airport?"

There you have it, some contextual attitudes that identify bad employees. These are extreme examples, a bit on the humorous side, but be assured that there are many potential employees who are just as bad and they are far less humorous. I have said it before but it applies here as well, *just because Ben Franklin wanted to make the turkey the national bird doesn't mean you have to hire one!*

The Big Nine Jerk Attitudes That Can Destroy a Workplace

Your goal is not to hire or promote a jerk. Just imagine, a jerk-free workplace. It almost sounds like the Beetle's song *Imagine* doesn't it? But this is a challenge. Most people think that the first line of defense against hiring a jerk is the job interview.

As mentioned before, interviews may not work when it comes to weeding out jerks. Does it surprise you that jerks can be very good at job interviews? Jerks can be charming upon first contact and very good at hiding their true attitudes. In fact, everyone is on their best behavior in a job interview--both the interviewer and the job applicant

A jerk is not going to say things like "I prefer to do as little as possible" or "I take offense easily" or "I wish I did not have to work." An interviewer is not going to say things like "You seem to be defensive" or "What is the real reason you have had so many jobs?" This is why weeding out jerks needs to go *beyond* traditional methods.

The Research

My research task was to learn a lot about jerks. In other words, learn what you want to avoid. You want to flush them out like a birddog and in this case you are hunting turkeys. I studied jerks in the workplace including embezzlers, back-stabbers, bad-mouthers, imposters, malcontents, chronic job-hoppers, and people who like to threaten others with lawsuits. I quickly learned that individuals in this Rogue's Gallery have bad attitudes in the extreme. Everyone has a bad day occasionally but these jerks make a lifestyle of it.

Part of my research included going to supervisors in various types of organizations and asking if it would be possible to interview some present or past employees about their work-related beliefs and attitudes. I didn't say I was looking for jerks and I interviewed all kinds of employees but, in truth, it was a turkey hunt. As a result of these interviews I identified nine attitudes as leading to potential workplace problems.

An instrument was then developed to measure the attitudes and it was validated by testing over 300 individuals from business, government, and associations. The scores were correlated with: the supervisors' rating of the individuals as far as disruptive behavior; number of jobs held in the past five years; and level of satisfaction with work. The correlations confirmed my hypotheses and persons with high scores (i.e. warning signals for jerk behavior) had more supervisor ratings indicating disruptive behavior, more job turnover, and more dislike of work in general.

I found that individuals in the Rogue's Gallery had bad attitudes in the extreme, and that these same bad attitudes were generally absent in good or non-disruptive employees.

I was also motivated by jury consultants who study human behavior to predict how jurors are likely to decide complicated issues. Jury consultants construct lengthy questionnaires for prospective jurors where they ask about values, beliefs, and attitudes. These are filters through which people interpret reality. They may ask "What do you think of the justice system?" and then "Why do you think that?" or "Why do you feel that way?" They also ask very specific questions such as the types of punishment the person believes in. These consultants have had much success in predicting behavior in the courtroom.

Next is the list of the nine attitudes that I identified as potentially leading to problems in the workplace. Note that each attitude is not a single dimension, rather it exists on a continuum. That is, each bad attitude that is related to disruptive behavior has a corresponding attitude that is related to getting along with people. The attitudes that can lead to problems are shown in bold.

The Nine Work-Related Attitudes

Judgmental versus accepting
Propensity to defend one's rights, a strong sense of right and wrong, may have the compulsion to intervene in a controversy. Tend to feel that rules are important and people are not.

Vindictive versus forgiving
Tends to keep track of obligations as well as perceived slights and insults, may persist in attempts to "get even."

Adversarial versus accommodating
Limited understanding of the needs and desires of other people and generally-accepted social obligations. May get satisfaction from confronting or hurting others.

Egocentric versus people oriented
May be disinclined to assist fellow workers, limited obligation to customers, and a general unwillingness to make sacrifices for the good of the organization.

Entitled versus unassuming
May assume that they are not being rewarded sufficiently, tends to see work as an obligation rather than an opportunity, and may have a sense of entitlement.

Undisciplined versus self-disciplined
Limited commitment to finish projects without supervision, has trouble concentrating and setting priorities, may not pull their weight as a team member.

Insubordinate versus respectful
Tends to doubt people in authority and the chain of command, may question that "rank has its privileges," oftentimes unwilling to seek help from a superior.

Risk-Inclined versus cautious
Generally unwilling to delay decisions in order to get more information, disinclined to check with others, and limited regard for record keeping.

Non-Traditional versus traditional
Oftentimes little desire to understand past events, rules and regulations, or work-related ceremonies.

The Man Who Inspired Me to Develop the Workplace Attitudes Test™

Some years ago *Reader's Digest* magazine had a section called "The Most Unforgettable Character I Ever Met." Well one of the most unforgettable characters I ever met was a man named Byron. (I changed the name here to protect the guilty.)

I first met Byron when he worked at a company where I was given a contract to do a research project for a few months. We became friends and over the years I saw a pattern develop -- he gets lots of jobs and leaves lots of jobs. I had a unique vantage point because I saw both sides of Byron, the work side and the personal side. Each time he got a new job, he would tell me why he did not like it and how he had a plan to leave the job with a big payoff. I saw the pain he caused his employers and I grew to disrespect him. I eventually started to think how I could develop a pre-employment test to help weed out people like Bryon and this lead to my developing the Workplace Attitudes Test.

The reason why Byron is so unforgettable is that he is the best job interviewer I have ever known. In the 20+ years I knew Byron he averaged at least three jobs a year. This would seem to be an undesirable situation but from Byron's point of view it works just fine. You see, Byron is not at all disinclined to threaten a lawsuit and his shell-shocked employer is often inclined to pay him off just to make the lawsuit and Byron go away.

Threats of Lawsuits

Now I suspect that you're a bit incredulous at this point. How would it be possible for someone to have over 60 jobs in 20 years? Why would someone even want to? Part of the answer is the threat of a lawsuit. The various settlements that Byron has collected over the years have resulted in a rather interesting career (a lot of time at the beach) for this skilled job interviewer. None have ever gone to court and it just took a few threatening letters in each situation for Byron to walk away with a big check.

Lots of Practice

I suppose Byron is very good at job interviewing because he has had a lot of practice and knows just what to say -- or rather, he knows just what you want to hear. Whatever you need, he is it. Byron establishes rapport with people when they can benefit him directly.

Charm

Byron portrays himself as a consultant to explain away his many jobs. He also has some rather impressive credentials including a Bachelor's and two Master's degrees, and has a few friends who feel pity for him and are usually willing to give him a decent recommendation where they imply he did some work for them. In fact, Byron is charming when you first meet him. To paraphrase a famous quote about Thomas Dewey, the politician, you have to really know Byron to dislike him.

A Chameleon

Byron is also a chameleon. You see Byron is Catholic, Protestant, Baptist, Jewish, and Agnostic. He has attended a Methodist Seminary, studied to be a Catholic priest, converted to Judaism, and explored his roots as a Baptist. He has left each of these religions and joined them again when convenient. When looking for a Catholic Monastery, he took trips around the country to find the one with the most money and offers. The one he finally chose paid off all his bills, bought his car, and paid for a Master's Degree, all in exchange for him becoming a priest. After two years, he had trouble with the vow of obedience and left. Then, after one year on his own, he was ready to return to the familiar cocoon where all needs were provided, but they turned him down! The head of the Monastery said he still believed that Byron had a problem with obedience even though Byron said he had changed.

Byron is from the Midwest, he is from Mississippi, he is from

Washington, D.C. and Colorado. He loves all sports and is quite conversant in a variety of subjects. He is also a member of various fraternal organizations and is great at networking. As friends and co-workers become inevitably disillusioned with him, he constantly finds new ones to replace them.

Some Byron Stories

In more than twenty years I never knew Byron to pay for a meal unless of course it was a very inexpensive meal to prime the pump for a better restaurant at someone else's expense. When visiting a friend, he never brings anything such as chips or beverages but before knocking on their door he will take something from the other visitor and present it as his own gift.

One boss asked Byron to write a press release and he refused saying he does not feel comfortable doing that. The boss also asked for his home number in case of an emergency and he also refused that request. The boss became increasingly frustrated and did not understand Byron's game and that he is a jerk. Byron had a master plan that he was putting into motion -- stay at the job for two or three months, do a poor job, get fired, threaten to sue because he felt he was not terminated fairly and request big walking-away money, then get a big check. He did this over and over for more than twenty years, and he got to spend a lot of time at the beach.

Work as Punishment

It should be obvious that once Byron gets a job he doesn't perform particularly well. In fact, he is quite disruptive. Of course, that is his intent. Basically, **he sees work as punishment**. He is probably the most entitled person I ever met. What is your defense against Byron? He'll tell you what you want to hear in the interview, has some good references, and unless you are lucky enough to run into one of his former employers and have a personal conversation, you are very likely to hire him. He takes your big checks to finance a life of little work, until he runs out of money and has to return to another gullible workplace for a little while. I hope you do not run into Byron!

As I mentioned, he was one of the inspirations for me to develop the Workplace Attitudes Test. I knew that if it worked with Byron, it stood the ultimate test. It turns out that Byron **scored very high on entitled and undisciplined**. Here are two warning signals and the test was clearly saying, "Don't hire him because there may be problems!"

Some people feel very entitled, others not at all. A strong sense of entitlement tends to make a person more difficult to work with. Problems arise because the highly entitled assume that they are not being sufficiently rewarded, they see work as an obligation rather than an opportunity, and they often feel put upon if they are asked to do anything extra. When combined with a high score on undisciplined, this mix becomes toxic.

So there you have it, "the most unforgettable character I ever met." In some ways I'm sorry that *Reader's Digest* doesn't still have this section. Our friend Byron certainly deserves the notoriety.

What I Could Have Called This Book

A book's title is very important. I spent a lot of time thinking about the title of this book. I wanted it to be humorous as well as informative and I wanted to describe the pre-employment test that I developed without being too technical. I think I can describe my intensions a little better if I tell you about the titles that I considered before selecting *Workplace Jerks! Will This Person be a Speed Bump, a Pothole or a Landmine?*

"Jerk Repellent: A Guide to Peace and Prosperity in the Workplace"

This title reflects the fact that you should develop a strategy to avoid hiring and promoting jerks. One jerk in the workplace can change the entire environment from one of cooperation and enthusiasm to frustration and disillusionment. A repellent is something that you use to keep insects or other pests away. Well this is what the Workplace Attitudes Test (WAT) does and the book is about what happens when your repellent doesn't work. Unfortunately the title is a little too lawn-and-garden. Plus it's a little bit harsh, implying that some people deserve to have repellent used on them. Accurate perhaps, but not politically correct.

"Certitude at Work: the Jerk Factor"

This title describes the predominant attitude of a lot of jerks and epitomizes one of my favorite quotes, "Seldom right but always certain." It brings to mind a strategy I sometimes use when confronted with someone who is what may be termed "boisterously certain." I sometimes say to them "I'm probably the wrong person to talk to because although I have no knowledge about this subject, I do have strong opinions!" Occasionally this stops them in their tracks. It's probably a good strategy but not so good for a book title. Most jerks are certain but it doesn't say much more about them.

"Be Thou Not a Jerk"

Now here's a title for those who are religiously inclined. It sounds a bit like one of the Ten Commandments and one that should probably have been included but it wasn't and so it is probably not a good title for a book.

"Testing for Jerks is Like Baking an Upside-Down Cake"

Now here's a title that gets to the heart of how the WAT was developed. Not a bad title because it tells how WAT is very different from other pre-employment test in the field -- it looks for bad attitudes while other tests look for desirable characteristics.

Remember Byron? He was good at being charming and appearing well-qualified for a job but this was surface only. Just under the surface was a caldron of bad attitudes including extreme entitlement and extreme lack of discipline. You would not know this without some type of attitude testing.

What we're looking for here are attitudes that are potentially disruptive. Why not look for what you are trying to avoid? That's what the test does. Unfortunately this title is a little too specific and it doesn't really say much about the workplace jerk problem in general. Plus, I thought it might end up in the cooking section of the library or bookstore. Hence it was discarded.

"How Can I Be a Jerk When I Know I'm Right?"

In a sense we're back at the certitude problem. This is a characteristic that makes jerks what they are but it is not overly descriptive and it leaves a lot of things out. It's catchy but it lacks something.

Workplace Jerks! Will This Person be a Speed Bump, a Pothole or a Landmine?

This is the title I selected and I hope you like it. I believe it is informative as well as humorous, and I like how it asks a question so you assume the author answers it in an interesting and unusual way.

Some Interesting Findings

As a result of my research, some interesting findings emerged that help answer the following questions. What does a jerk look like? Will jerks answer questions honestly? What percent of people in the workplace are jerks?

What Does a Jerk Look Like?

A jerk is someone who is disruptive in the workplace. They can be rude to customers and difficult to work with. They tend to have low social skills and my assumption is the workplace is a social environment. They tend to be abusive and unfortunately can sometimes be found in positions of authority. Everyone has a bad day occasionally but jerks are consistent.

Jerks are everywhere. They are in blue-collar jobs and white-collar jobs. They are in factories and in offices. They are on the roads and in stores. You have probably experienced a cashier who was talking on their cell phone to a friend while also helping you and dealing with money. Last week I got some help, grudgingly, from a clerk at Radio Shack who was on her cell phone the entire time. She was having two conversations at the same time, one with me and one with a company on the other end of the phone about a bill she was paying.

Generally, I have found that jerks at work have an overall lack of gratitude. They are not grateful for having employment, for having friends at work, for doing a good job. It is possible that they see work as punishment.

They do not play by the same rules as the rest of us. Oftentimes, they are proud of their attitudes and during my interviews they said things such as:

"Most people are stupid."
"You can't trust anybody."

"Work is a pain in the neck but you have to do it."
"Step on my toes and I won't forget it."

In essence, they tend not to see themselves as the problem -- it is always someone else's fault.

Will Jerks Answer Honestly?

When I began asking respondents about their attitudes, I was concerned that they may not want to admit to having such strong values or beliefs.

For example, take the following options:

Q. When someone insults or slights me . . . (select one of the following answers)

A. I tend to remember it a very long time.
B. I can hold a grudge, but not often.
C. at first I get irritated, but soon forget it.

Turns out, I did not need to be concerned because they do select some extreme answers. In this case, the extreme answer is "A." In follow-up interviews I discovered that people with strong or extreme attitudes are proud of these attitudes. They tend to believe in absolutes. Later, correlating extreme answers with job performance suggested that attitudinal rigidity does incline a person to disruptive behavior.

If you listen carefully you can often hear, "You've got to watch your back all the time," or "It's a dog-eat-dog world out there." Yep, people will tell you what they really think if you just give them a chance.

Skilled interviewers can sometimes pick up on attitudinal rigidity but most often the interviewer concentrates on "can do the job" rather than "will do the job." Also many interviewers may feel it is not polite to ask these types of questions. That is why the Workplace Attitudes Test is so valuable. It asks questions that you may not be inclined to ask face-to-face, and my findings show that people are willing to answer accurately.

What Percent of People Are Jerks?

Once people learn that I have some expertise about jerks in the workplace, I am often asked, "What percent of employees have problem attitudes?" This is difficult to answer with precision. I would say that usually among a group of job applicants, approximately one out of twenty has at least one high warning signal on the test. This usually comes as a surprise to interviewers who find it difficult to identify these problem attitudes in a regular job interview.

One of my basic assumptions is if you avoid hiring problem employees, by default you will hire good employees. This is very important if you consider that a jerk supervisor who does hiring is likely to hire other jerks, or the attitudes of one jerk at the top of an organization may set the tone for the entire place. In other words, jerks can be disruptive *all out of proportion* to their numbers.

Jerks need to be avoided at all levels. Corporate Boards should not tolerate them. Government regulators should regulate them. Legislators should make laws to punish them. President Madison said, "If men were angels, government would not be necessary." Rules and consideration for one's fellow man should apply to everyone.

Ain't Human Nature Funny

In this chapter I start by summarizing two stories I read about the importance of attitude. The first is a parable that shows how a bad attitude, or good attitude, can determine our path in life. The second is from a short story that shows how a desire to help others comes from your inner attitudes and is not based on receiving thanks, recognition, or something in return. Then I move on to famous wits, turkeys, and Charlie Brown.

A Fork in the Road

There is a parable about an old gent who lived near a fork in the road. Let's give him a long white beard and assume that he was very wise. I'll call him Oscar. Oscar liked to sit near the road smoking his meerschaum pipe filled with happy-go-lucky brand tobacco and passers-by would ask him about what it was like in the next town. Well, granting that Oscar was near a fork in the road, there were two towns ahead but it didn't really matter because the conversation was always pretty much the same.

When someone asked, "What are the people like in the next town?" Oscar replied by asking "What were the people like in the last town?"

They would say "They were mean and unpleasant, that's why I am moving on" or they would say, "I loved those people and I hate to move."

Oscar would reply, often in a cloud of smoke, "Well, I think you'll find the folks in the next town pretty much the same."

I call Oscar wise because he was always right. I think it had something to do with understanding the importance of attitude.

No Good Deed Goes Unpunished

I have often wondered about this expression. Apparently, it is cross-cultural and quite old. One of my hobbies is showing that everyone is an idiot in all languages other than their own. Thus, as an exercise in humility, I spend time reading rudimentary Spanish.

I recently ran across a short story called "Carta a Dios" (Letter to God) written in 1940 by the Mexican writer Gregorio Lopez y Fuentes. (For those readers who are conversant in Spanish please place the missing accents where they belong.) This charming vignette illustrates a fundamental fact about human nature, i.e. if you know what someone takes for granted or what they accept to be true without question, you know that which is most important about them. Some of you cynics out there will note that this story also shows that "No good deed goes unpunished."

But on with the story. Our protagonist is a dirt-poor peasant named Lencho. The scene: a small house on a hill near a river, a corral, and a small field of corn and beans soon ready for harvest but in need of rain. Lencho's wife calls her husband and their two sons from the fields and their youngest boy from nearby to a simple dinner.

Conversation turns to the weather and the clouds descending from the northeast that promise rain. Lencho asserts "Soon it is going to rain" and his wife adds, "God willing." And so it rains, the harvest is good, and Lencho and his family live happily ever after. Not really!

Instead it hails, the leaves are stripped off the trees, the land is covered with salt-like crystals of ice, the crop is ruined and the family is devastated. No one can help Lencho and his family and they are destined to starve the following year. But Lencho is a man of faith and asserts, "Surely, God will not let us starve."

Although Lencho worked like a beast of burden all his life, somehow he learned to write and so he decides to write a letter to God. He writes, "God, if you do not help, we will die of hunger this coming year. I need one hundred pesos to plant another crop and to live until the harvest comes in."

Lencho puts his letter in an envelope, addresses it to "God," goes to the post office, buys a stamp and puts it into the mailbox. Sometime later a postal employee sees the letter, opens it and chuckles. He shows it to his supervisor who also laughs and then becomes serious. He says, "Such simple faith is a beautiful thing to see. We cannot disillusion a man of such faith." And so the supervisor takes part of his paycheck and asks his fellow employees and their friends for contributions.

Although they cannot collect all of the one hundred pesos they are able to enclose sixty. They put the money in an envelope with Lencho's name on it. Lencho arrives a few days later and asks if there is a letter for him. He exhibits not the least surprise when he is told yes. Ah, such faith.

Lencho opens the envelope, counts the money and becomes infuriated. He goes to the post office window, asks for paper and pen, and writes the following, "God, the money that I asked for arrived in my hands with only sixty pesos. Send the rest because it is much needed, but don't send it to this post office because all of the employees who work here are crooks. Lencho."

Wits, Pundits and Famous
People Talk About Jerks

First, a jerk definition from Forbes. I was recently surfing the Internet and found that the Forbes publishing empire spends a lot of time and ink on discussing jerks and how to deal with them so I suppose their definition is as good a definition as any. This comes from www.Forbes.com/2006.

"Jerks are people whose behavior is so inappropriate and outrageous that it creates problems for everyone near them. Jerks can be managers, co-workers, clients, male or female, young or old, well educated or a dropout. Jerkdom knows no bounds."

Comedians and pundits have a lot to say about jerks. Sometimes I think that one of the best things about jerks is that they inspire comedians. For example **Groucho Marx** facetiously self-identified when he said "I wouldn't belong to any club that would have me as a member." **Will Rogers** is described in Wikipedia as a Cherokee cowboy, comedian, humorist, social commentator, vaudeville performer and actor. He once said "When our district sent a representative to the U.S. Congress, it raised the IQ of both places." But let's move on, it seems a little too easy to take potshots at politicians.

Probably my favorite jerk put-down was said by **Lee Marvin** in the movie *Paint Your Wagon*, where he insulted a jerk by saying, "When I was conceived my parents did not have the benefit of marriage but you sir are a self-made man."

Gore Vidal proved that he could be a bit of a jerk when he said "It is not enough for me to succeed, it is necessary for my enemies to fail." **Lady Astor** was known for her biting wit. She said to **Winston Churchill** "If I were married to you, I would put poison in your tea." Wrong target. Churchill replied "If I were married to you, madam, I would drink it."

Mr. Churchill also described one of his political opponents by saying "He is a modest man but then he has much to be modest about." Another Brit, **Sydney Smith** (1771–1845) said to someone "What you don't know would fill a book."

The comedic put down of jerks has a long history. In fact, one of the favorite themes in literature is the story of how a jerk gets his comeuppance. One of the most famous novels to carry out this theme is the *Count of Monte Cristo* by **Andre Dumas**. It is a story about a man who is defrauded, then discovers a treasure which makes him rich and thus he is able to get back at his enemies.

Unfortunately, this takes place years ago in France and not on present-day Wall Street. But everyone on Wall Street is not a jerk, and being a jerk once in a while doesn't make you one.

Now, you have probably noticed that I have ended some sentences in this book with a preposition. That reminds me of the old joke about the tourist who visits Harvard University and asks "Excuse me sir, can you please tell me where the library is at?" The Harvard man replies, "We at Harvard do not end a sentence with a preposition." The tourist says, "Oh, I'm sorry, can you tell me where the library is at, asshole?"

Turkeys Are Not Grateful

When I did the initial research to discover attitudes related to disruptive behavior in the workplace, I had the opportunity to meet a lot of jerks, sometimes referred to as "turkeys."

My good friend Tom Gorski has a wonderful talent for drawing cartoons and I am grateful to him for the turkey you see in this book.

The research helped me develop the Workplace Attitudes Test but if you decide that a pre-employment test that measures attitudes is not for you, I suggest that you look for gratitude. Gratitude explains a lot. If you find evidence of gratitude, I believe you have a good chance of finding a person who will get along well with others.

Gratitude can come in various forms such as:

I am grateful to have a job.

I am grateful for my family.

I am grateful to live in a free country.

I am grateful for my friends.

I am grateful for my health.

I am grateful that I am a person who can feel joy.

I am grateful for my education.

I am grateful to my parents for all they provided me.

I am grateful for the animals in my life such as my dog, cat, horse, pig, or goat.

Wikipedia provides the following definition:

"Gratitude, thankfulness, or appreciation is a positive emotion or attitude in acknowledgment of a benefit that one has received or will receive."

One of my favorite quotes on this subject is by Meister Eckhart and is found at www.wisdomquotescom.

"If the only prayer you said in your whole life was, 'thank you,' that would suffice."

At the same web site, Melodie Beattie eloquently talks about gratitude as follows.

"Gratitude unlocks the fullness of life. It turns what we have into enough, and more. It turns denial into acceptance, chaos into order, confusion into clarity . . . It turns problems into gifts, failures into success, the unexpected into perfect timing, and mistakes into important events. Gratitude makes sense of our past, brings peace for today and creates a vision for tomorrow."

The singer Willie Nelson says:

"I am not cold. I am not hungry. And neither are you."

To summarize, I say that if you are looking for an employee who will get along well with other people and you do not want to use a measurement test, you probably can't go wrong by asking them *"What are you grateful for?"*

Sometimes "Lucy" Was a Jerk but Charles Schultz Seldom Was: Optimism versus Cynicism

Charles Schultz, the famous cartoonist and I might add philosopher, was once asked, "How optimistic are you about the future of America?" After all, Charlie Brown, his erstwhile protagonist suffered an inordinate amount of frustration. Year after year Lucy would promise to hold the football only to yank it away at the last moment. Suffering catastrophe after catastrophe, a disillusioned Charlie would utter, "Good Grief."

Nevertheless, concerning optimism and America, Mr. Schultz was very optimistic. When asked why, he said because every day millions of hard-working Americans went to work, did their job, took care of their children and met their obligations. The simple fact is the vast majority of people do us proud.

The anecdotal evidence suggests that there are a lot of turkeys out there and you probably ran into one or two this week. Most people do follow the rules, are invariably polite, and are easy to get along with. Unfortunately, it is the turkeys that have a disproportionate impact, and sometimes managers must spend considerable time reigning in the five percent so that the other ninety-five percent don't get totally disgusted.

I believe that the opposite of optimism is cynicism. There is a type of jerk who is a cynic or critic. I like the quote by H.L. Mencken, "A cynic is a man who, when he smells flowers, looks around for a coffin." Can a cynic change? It is hard to say. It takes some introspection and a desire to see things differently.

Alright I admit it, I like self-help books. They might be a bit self-delusional but I think they do a lot of good. What's wrong with someone deciding that they need improvement and some inspiration to go about the task? Even Ben Franklin made a list of things to improve on. At the very least, self-help efforts are good antidotes to smug people who feel that life is full of certainty.

Sure, Einstein probably didn't read self-help books but he had the intellectual tools to begin with. The rest of us probably could use the boost.

Some Theories About Jerks

Jerks and Gamesmanship

In 1964 Eric Berne wrote a book called *Games People Play*. Later, he wrote a book called *What Do You Say After You Say Hello?* Dr. Berne was a psychiatrist in the tradition of Sigmund Freud and he founded a school of psychology known as Transactional Analysis.

These books were clearly written and quite popular with the public. Unfortunately, some academics in the field looked down at any books that had a popular following and they derided Transactional Analysis as "pseudo-science." Dr. Berne's first book used Transactional Analysis to explain games people play.

I suggest that one of the games played by the critics could have been termed "I don't care what your credentials say, I'm an expert and you're not!"

Albeit, I believe that Transactional Analysis can be very useful to both psychotherapy and understanding jerks. In fact psychotherapy may not be such a bad idea for some jerks.

Transactional Analysis

I won't go into great detail about Transactional Analysis and here is a brief summary. Dr. Berne states that at any given time, a person experiences and manifests their personality through a mixture of behaviors, thoughts, and feelings. He notes that there are three ego states that people consistently use. These are called Parent ("extero-psyche"), Adult ("neo-psyche), and Child ("archaeo-psyche").

The terms, Parent, Adult, and Child have specific definitions that are shown below. In some ways it is unfortunate that Dr. Berne chose these terms instead of obfuscatory academic lingo. Then he might have been taken more seriously by the experts.

Parent states are where people behave, feel, and think in response to just mimicking how their parents (or parental figures) acted or how they interpreted the actions of their parents. For example a person may shout out of frustration because they saw an influential figure (parent) do this and it seemed to work.

Adult states are most like computers processing information. This suggests that adult states are "rational and objective" rather than "emotional."

Child states are where people behave, feel, and think in ways similar to what they did in childhood.

Dr. Berne does not make value statements about each of these ego states. For example, he notes that the Child is the source of emotions, creativity, recreation, spontaneity and intimacy.

He does use the states to explain how people interact and sometimes play games. These games can be very useful for understanding jerk behavior and I describe a few of them below. The name of each game is in bold letters and is from Dr. Berne, and an example of each is from my own writing.

"Now I've got you, you SOB" (NIGYYSOB)

This game has an aggressor and a victim. Basically, the aggressor puts the victim in situations where he or she says the victim is always wrong. Hence the name, "Now I've got you, you SOB." It is a power play that seems to be particularly entertaining for some jerk bosses. Instead of win-win, it has to be win-lose.

For example, the boss gives you a task and says it will last at least two weeks, then after one week asks you for the results.

You can mumble that you are sorry and say you need another week. If you're lucky, the righteous boss says "Well, just don't do it again, too bad it is taking so long" and this could be the end of the game. But oftentimes the game goes on, depending on how sadistic your boss happens to be.

For example you can explain that the job is going to take at least two weeks and your boss can say "You should have said that when I gave you the assignment." Or the boss can say, "Why didn't you ask for help when I gave you the assignment?" In your defense you can say "I didn't know that you needed it so soon." Of course, your boss says "You should have told me, I can't read your mind."

I think you get the idea, that you can't win this one. The best you can do is to recognize the situation for what it is -- a game. As a strategy, all you can do is to try to keep the game as short as possible.

"Why don't you? Yes but" (WDYYB)

This is a game most often played between colleagues. Basically one person poses a problem and a second person offers solutions but the first person rejects each solution. They always find a flaw in all the proposed solutions and this game continues until both parties become frustrated. In the workplace it can be played endlessly with a variety of topics. The person asking for help can go from person to person and reject all of their ideas until everyone becomes very frustrated.

Then, oftentimes, they go back to the first person and start all over again. You can easily see why this game affects productivity. Here's an example of how the game works.

First person (FP): I need to get a college degree.
Second person (SP): Hey that sounds great, why don't you enroll at the state University?

FP: **Yes but** the tuition is more than I can afford right now.
SP: Well, you can go to a community college because their tuition is quite low.

FP: **Yes but** I have my heart set on a major university.
SP: I have an idea, you can go to night school at the university.

FP: **Yes but** I hate to go out at night. Besides, my neighborhood is not safe at night.
SP: Oh, they have classes on the weekend.

FP: **Yes but** my weekends are pretty packed.
SP: You know that they have online classes.

FP: **Yes but** my computer is kind of old so I'm not sure it would work that well.
SP: Hey, I have an extra computer you can borrow.

FP: **Yes but** I hate to take on the responsibility of borrowing your computer.

"Why Don't You? Yes But" can go on indefinitely. What is the gain for the first person? Well the first person gets to stump people. Also, this person gets to demonstrate that their problem is "insoluble" thus justifying their lack of trying a new endeavor.

"Why does this always happen to me?" (WAHM)

I suppose this could be a country western song, something like "My house burned down, my horse is dead, and my wife is gone. Oh, why does this always happen to me?"

Now, I'm not minimizing real tragedies and the need to commiserate with people who have problems. However, "Why does this always happen to me" is a way of life for some people. They spend a great deal of time and effort describing why you should feel sorry for them. This can be anywhere from complaining about a bad hangover, not having enough money, or hating life in general.

You have to make a decision as to whether you wish to commiserate with this type of person. They will probably call you insensitive or non-caring but I assure you, if you refuse to play this game you will save a lot of time and heartache. You get all the heartache you need from country western songs.

"Ain't it awful?" (AIA)

This game has a lot in common with "Why does this always happen to me." This game is often played in governmental terms. For example, the government is too oppressive, the budget is too high, or politicians and all government are no damn good. There is also a variation known as "Remember the good old days." For example, "I remember when shoes only cost a dollar and you could depend on your horse. That was before the dumb computers took over."

"Let's you and him fight" (LYAHF)

Dr. Berne describes "Let's you and him fight" as primarily a romantic game that involves a triangle and says it often happens in literature where a woman maneuvers or challenges two men to fight over her with the implication or promise that she will pledge herself to the winner.

What about triangles in the workplace? Some jerks use triangles to maneuver themselves into favorable positions. Let's look at three people and call them Slim, Stubby, and Bob. Bob decides to pit the other two against each other. He is the instigator and then plays the role of the arbitrator and the game goes something like this.

Bob says: "Slim, I think Stubby is saying bad things behind your back."

Bob then says: "Stubby, it seems that Slim is saying some weird things about you."

When Slim and/or Stubby come to Bob, he continues the game by confirming their suspicions. This allows Bob to have all sorts of "fun" at the expense of both Slim and Stubby and also be the center of attention. Certain types of people seem to enjoy this game and it can result in considerable havoc in the workplace.

I have often wondered about the etiology of this behavior and I suspect it comes from patterns developed in early childhood. Some children learn to pit one parent against another to get what they want. For example, a child may ask a father for a candy bar and if he says no, then the child goes to the mother with the same request and she says yes.

If the parents fight over this issue, the child becomes the center of attention. According to Dr. Berne's game theory, this type of behavior, when rewarded in childhood, becomes a behavioral pattern later in life.

You can just imagine the type of havoc that these triangle strategies can create in a workplace environment.

Jerks and Dangerous Behavior

Temper Tantrums

We have all heard the expression "going postal" and it describes a very real danger in the workplace. This expression unfortunately maligns hard-working postal workers and frankly gives them a bad rap. Nevertheless, "going postal" describes the potentially-dangerous situation of violence in the workplace.

In 1812 Lady Caroline Lamb famously described Lord Byron, who was a man of great excesses, as "mad, bad and dangerous to know" and this rings true today in many situations. Paula Hodges, who writes articles for the web site www.helium.com, says "A temper tantrum occurs when a person (regardless of age) releases all control. They then scream, call names, throw things, whatever, in an attempt to get what they want."

Addressing the problem of temper tantrums can be quite a challenge. When someone is having a tantrum, they are not rational.

Psychiatrist Sydney Friedman in the hit TV series MASH, described someone he thought was a jerk by saying "He is such a sack of fertilizer it is hard to care." Wouldn't it be nice if it were that simple? Unfortunately, with a boss or a co-worker who is a jerk you have a serious problem.

As a first step, I think you're going to have to assess how much of an out-of-control jerk this person really is. Remember the title of this book, *Workplace Jerks! Will This Person be a Speed Bump, a Pothole or a Landmine?* Well, in terms of temper tantrums, what are they? If they're a speed bump, maybe they just lose their temper once in a while and you can tolerate it. If they're a pothole, maybe you can work around the situation. If they're an out-of-control landmine, well there is little you can do and you might want to consider a transfer.

Basically you've got to remember that if the person is your boss, they have a canon and you have the pop-gun. Sometimes you can bring in reinforcements by telling their boss, but this is risky. There could be retaliation by the jerk.

According to Melody Chase, another writer at www.helium.com, there are five possible reasons for adult tantrums.

1) It is the only way they know how to get their needs met.

2) They have learned that life is all about survival. They believe they need to fight and be aggressive because they believe the world is not abundant in that there are limited resources.

3) They have a trigger. That is, there is something that makes them react all out of proportion to the situation.

4) Their personality is more predisposed to getting angry or blowing up. For example, they may have what is termed a Driver Personality. These individuals are bottom-line, goal oriented, bossy, and sometimes rude.

5) Finally, they may have a medical condition or may be exhausted.

Paula Hodges makes the following suggestion concerning tantrums: "It would take me less than 5 seconds to tap 3 keys on my cell phone to make a video, (complete with sound) of such an event." She goes on to say that she could not imagine anyone in a position of authority who would enjoy seeing a playback of something like this. Well I'm not so sure, it may be the best way to get your phone smashed. Just a thought.

For speed bumps and potholes there are a few strategies. For example, you can ask "how can I help solve the situation?" You can try not to take it personally. You can ask for clarification. However, landmine jerks are a different matter and may require professional intervention.

Sexual Harassment

It is impossible to talk about jerks without saying something about sexual harassment. If a jerk does get sued, this may be the cause. There are laws to protect and empower the victims. I'm reminded of the quote found in the book, *Catcher in the Rye*. A character in the book describes someone as "having the sensitivity of a toilet seat" and that can really describe a jerk. Sexual harassment should not be tolerated in the work environment. End of discussion.

For more information about the laws and regulations go to the web site of the U.S. Equal Employment Opportunity Commission at www.eeoc.gov. It has Fact Sheets that explain the laws and regulations in simple terms and it covers discrimination by: age; disability; genetic information; national origin; pregnancy; race/color; religion; retaliation; sex; and sexual harassment. Your workplace should have this information posted on a board for all to see.

The EEOC Fact Sheet on sexual harassment says:

"Although the law doesn't prohibit simple teasing, offhand comments, or isolated incidents that are not very serious, harassment is illegal when it is so frequent or severe that it creates a hostile or offensive work environment or when it results in an adverse employment decision (such as the victim being fired or demoted)."

Threats and Lawsuits

Sometimes jerks get their way by threatening lawsuits. (This is very different from filing a legitimate lawsuit.) Jerks know that one letter from an attorney is often all it takes for an employer to cave in and pay the jerk to go away. The employer knows that the cost of defending their company can run into hundreds of thousands of dollars, incredible stress, and lots of time away from the company. This is the way it is in the United States. It may be different in other countries where there is loser-pay, i.e. if you lose the lawsuit you have to pay all the costs of both sides. I believe that loser-pay makes people think twice before threatening a lawsuit and that it leads to fewer lawsuits overall.

I describe jerks who file lawsuits in two chapters. The chapter entitled "The Man Who Inspired Me to Develop the Workplace Attitudes Test" describes a man who sees work as punishment. His solution is to get a job, keep it for a few months, intentionally get terminated, then threaten to sue for wrongful termination, and receive a big check to drop the lawsuit. He has done this dozens of times over many years.

The chapter entitled "Guesstimating the Cost of Hiring a Jerk" has a description of a company with two jerks who wanted to sell a product they did not own. Another man named Jim invented the product and owned the registered trademarks that covered it. Instead of paying Jim for the rights to sell the product, they decided to sue him. They figured that Jim could not afford a lawsuit, would not show up to defend himself, and would therefore lose the suit by default meaning they could have the product. Jim surprised them and fought the lawsuit but it cost him $100,000. Later, he found out that this is a strategy the two jerks use over and over again. Bottom line, they use intimidation as a weapon.

Believing the World is a Dangerous Place

Jerks always seem to be mad. Theirs is what may be termed a zero-sum world. It's as if they're playing poker all the time. For them to win, someone else has to lose. I'm reminded of that old country western song "I don't like it but I guess things happen that way." We all know people who make themselves feel more important by tearing others down. Some people do this because they actually feel inferior or inadequate. These jerks can be even more dangerous in powerful government positions because with an attitude like this, a powerful government leader could take his or her country to an unnecessary war.

Unfortunately, dangerous behavior also occurs in schools and a young, desperate person who is the subject of bullying can react in many ways. More and more schools are developing policies against bullying and are training students in ways to avoid it. An organization with more information about school programs in the area of bullying is Family, Career and Community Leaders of America (FCCLA) and their web site is www.fccla.org. Their program is called *Stop the Violence*.

Another source of information is the American Psychological Association. Their web site at www.apa.org has information on bullying and related workplace issues.

An article in *Parade Magazine* in 2010 is entitled "Workplace Bullying: Do We Need a Law?" It says that according to the polling firm Zogby and the Workplace Bullying Institute (WBI), an employee-advocacy group, nearly fifty percent of the U.S. workforce is a victim of or a witness to bullying on the job. WBI defines this as "repeated malicious mistreatment, verbal abuse, or conduct that is threatening, humiliating, or intimidating, or that interferes with work."

Workplace Policy

Companies should have a place where policies are clearly posted for all to see. This can include Standards of Behavior and what is not tolerated. It should also have information from the Equal Employment Opportunity Commission that defines harassment and retaliation and the laws that protect individuals in the workplace. Better yet, this information should also be part of packets given to new employees.

Companies have some tools to protect themselves from jerks such as putting new hires on probation, and taking all complaints seriously. Remember that the workplace culture in any organization usually comes from the top down. Ultimately, it is the responsibility of the CEO to set the standards and disseminate them.

Federal government agencies have an EEOC Officer who can research the complaints on behalf of employees who believe they have been hurt, and then file claims with the EEOC. They also have

Inspectors General who handle extremely sensitive matters such as whistleblowers. There are laws to protect whistleblowers but many still lose their job. As I am writing this, there is a story in the news about a whistleblower at Arlington National Cemetery who lost her job after she went to her boss and complained about grave sites having the wrong names on them, or worse, and records being in disarray. Fortunately, she later found a job in another government agency.

Some Personal Experiences and Observations

Jerk Supervisors

We've all encountered jerks in the workplace; sometimes as a customer, sometimes with a fellow worker, and sometimes under the suzerainty of an unreasonable supervisor.

It is important to remember jerks sometimes tend to congregate together and one jerk inside your organization may lead to others especially if they are a supervisor who does hiring. Sometimes a CEO, VP, or Director is a jerk and their attitudes permeate the culture of an entire organization. Their attitudes can flow downward, affect everyone, and even affect policy. There can often be a multiplier effect when it comes to jerks and this means it is doubly important to avoid them.

There is no question that one problem employee can pollute the workplace and it can be worse if that one person is a supervisor. You have probably witnessed a workplace that was happy, and then with a change in managers became a neurosis-driven dysfunctional environment.

It is possible that government agencies, schools, and non-profit organizations have their own ways to deal with jerks and can afford to take some time to deal with them. This may also be true of large businesses. But what about smaller businesses who oftentimes depend on a small profit to keep going? How long can they tolerate a jerk?

I am thinking of a sewing and fabric store that had a low-key, tolerant supervisor who was primarily concerned with keeping customers happy. As often happens, this manager was promoted and replaced by an individual with a different agenda. Neatness was the new top priority of the new manager. Scraps of fabric on the floor were not tolerated and employees had to pick up scraps of cloth while customers were ignored. When the scraps were gone, then bolts of fabric needed to be folded properly at all times. Customer complaints increased because they felt they were being ignored, all the employees were blamed and made to sign statements acknowledging the problems, and longtime employees quit. Hello neatness, goodbye profits. A year later this chain of stores was in bankruptcy although they were able to reorganize and start anew.

Workplaces are social environments and it is essential that everyone works well together as a happy team. Ninety-five percent of the employees can be good but that ain't enough. All it takes is one jerk

A Blockbuster Experience

Last year I received a phone call from Blockbusters. It was a recording saying that I failed to return one of their movies. I had returned it to the store a few days earlier and since the message did not include a return phone number I decided to stop by the store to explain the situation. It was not a store that I normally use but it was near a fast food restaurant I like so I thought I would try the single stone/two-bird gambit.

Now, as you may know, Blockbuster does not give you a receipt when you return a movie. It's sort of "on the honor system" and one has to hope for the best. When I arrived at the store I waited patiently while the solo employee finished a phone conversation on the merits of various ski resorts. I thought my patience would be rewarded with a modicum of empathy. After waiting at the cash register for a time, the employee looked at me with a trace of annoyance and asked "What can I do for you?" I explained that I had received a phone call saying that I had not returned a movie but that, in fact, I had. This explanation was rewarded by a blank stare and the words, "Your card." I immediately interpreted this as meaning my Blockbuster card and I handed it over.

A quick swipe of the card into their computer system indicated that I must be a kleptomaniac with a tendency for mendacity. I was told

"Our records show that the movie was not returned." I said that I returned the movie a few days ago. He repeated, "Our records show that the movie was not returned." It appeared that we were in a bit of a loop.

This was an older movie and the store only had one. I asked, "Could you check the shelves?" He said, "You could." After two minutes of frantic looking, I found the movie and brought it to the counter. In a moment of contrition only found in some prison cell blocks, the clerk said, "Lucky you." The clerk then turned his back to make another phone call.

I suspect that this person would score quite high on more than one of the warning signals of the Workplace Attitudes Test (WAT). I got to thinking, how much money does this type of employee cost Blockbusters?

In the future I don't want this kind of surprise. I like to know what to expect. Unless they embrace truth in advertising and change their name to Ballbusters, I won't be back to this particular store.

Now I'm not a very good movie-rental customer but I often bought a snack or even a book at this store, so each visit to this store totaled about $10 or more. In a year I might spend about $300 in the store. Not a lot of money but it can add up fast, especially if other people have similar experiences.

A McDonalds Experience

Contrast this with another shopping experience. I was waiting in line at McDonalds to purchase and scarf down one of their vaulted chicken wraps when a rather disheveled octogenarian lady cut in front of me. She asked for a coke and the cash register rang up $1.06. She took out a shabby coin purse and slowly counted out 76 cents. Alas, she had no more and looked up expectantly at the cashier who smiled sympathetically. The cashier said "That's okay" and gave her a cup for her coke.

After the lady left, the cashier was obviously concerned that I had to wait and said "I'm sorry." I said "That's all right" but before I could give my order, the octogenarian was back. Looking confused, she said, "I want ice cream." The ice cream machine was broken and I could see my snack wrap fading into the sunset. The cashier said "Ma'am we have apple pie, would you like apple pie?" Now you may have heard the expression "No good deed goes unpunished." The old woman said, "I'd like two" and the cashier replied, "Two it is."

When the cashier got back to me, she again apologized. I got my order and also gave the cashier extra change to pay for the old woman. I did this because I can be very generous when it comes to small amounts and someone was probably watching. I am reminded of one of my favorite expressions, "There is no greater pleasure than to do an anonymous good deed and then to get caught!"

This is a store where the employees and managers are always happy and greet everyone with a smile. Maybe this is why I return there often. I even look forward to going there!

If you would like to hire the second employee rather than the first (at Blockbuster), and increase your profits, maybe you should consider better screening methods when hiring or promoting.

Jack the Embezzler

Now I knew Jack was an embezzler. In fact he had just spent about two years in the pokey for "borrowing" money from a business where he was employed. I knew this because a dear friend of mine knew Jack and asked me to give him a second chance. I agreed and since my small research company was fairly new at the time I figured there wasn't that much to steal. I also told Jack that he was being hired on a conditional basis.

Jack looked good, chiseled Grecian features, $500 suits, alligator shoes, and a really nice brief case. I hired him on a Friday and by the following Monday he had read all of our reports and promotional material and was quite well informed. Jack appeared to do a very good job and I was, frankly, impressed.

As I mentioned, there was very little opportunity to misappropriate funds but my small research company did have an asset that seemed to have moderate value. We had done some research for a local airline and they paid us in trade-out. This trade-out was like a promissory note that could be used for various services such as airline tickets, restaurant meals, and hotel accommodations.

Soon Jack learned about our trade-out account and asked me for a "small" favor. He had a girlfriend who had helped him when he needed a friend and he would like to take her to a local ski resort for the weekend to reward her.

I mean, how could I refuse? How much could he spend on two nights at a local ski resort? I made it part of his pay and I figured it might amount to a few hundred dollars.

The trade-out account had $7,000 in it and Jack and his girlfriend spent it all in two days. Of course, I didn't know this until I tried to use the account a few weeks later and by that time, Jack had another job with a large advertising agency. Apparently, it is easier for a person with a job to find another job when he already has one. This is probably especially true for an embezzler. On the plus side, this was one of the experiences that encouraged me to study jerks in the workplace.

Gloria the Drama Queen

I have come to the conclusion that I am a lousy interviewer. I have hired some real turkeys. I remember thinking what nice people they seemed to be in the interview. One turned out to be a drama queen whom I will call Gloria. Of course, at the time, I didn't know that she was a drama queen. After all, she made it obvious in the interview that she thought I was clever and intelligent and that counts for a lot.

Later, when I developed the WAT she agreed to take the test. The results showed that she is -- well, a drama queen. She tested very high on entitled, undisciplined, and insubordinate but what did I know?

Now I consider the WAT the best darn bad-attitude screening device available today, and Gloria and Jack deserve some of the credit for inspiring me to develop it.

Gloria did some part-time work for my company for a few months and then moved on when she found a full-time job. Gloria makes a good first impression because she has seemingly good social skills which are important in an interview. On the job, she is a disaster. She cannot focus because she prefers to talk and socialize, and she quickly ignores the chain of command. She often fails to do her job or finish a project and always blames someone else. In other words, her survival skills are highly developed and she has a tendency to scapegoat people.

Supervising Gloria became a Herculean task for her new boss, who confided in me. Picture this -- she was on several committees, interacted with almost everybody, especially the higher-ups, and she saw work as party time. Several of her colleagues and her immediate boss became fed up with her but by then she had friends in all the right places.

It took over a year but after countless intrigue, much of it orchestrated by Gloria herself, she was finally encouraged to move on. And if you don't want to fire someone like Gloria, you give her a good recommendation to make sure that she moves on. Did I mention that one of the people that Gloria befriended was the organization's legal counsel? He thought a good recommendation might be wise. Of course, one can't outright lie but everyone agreed that Gloria has great people skills.

Deep Do-Do on Wall Street

Ah, irony of ironies. Here I have developed a pre-employment instrument that is designed to screen out low- and mid-level people who are likely to be jerks in the workplace while at the highest level, the pigs have taken over the farm, the fox has been put in charge of the hen house, and the engineers have been asleep at the switch. Are these too many clichés? Give me a break, how in hell can I describe the imbroglio called Wall Street and the housing meltdown that started in 2008?

Yes, the WAT will help you keep jerks out of the workplace but short of a revolution, what do we do about sociopathic executives and irresponsible regulators? Frankly, I just don't know.

Maybe one possible answer is to teach ethics in MBA programs, as well as some financial history and political science. Those on Wall Street are entrusted with great responsibility and they need to understand . . .

1) financial mistakes of the past. (Housing prices have not always gone up as many people who lived through the 1980's in the west and southwest U.S. can explain);

2) human nature is fallible. (Some regulation is needed to curb out-of-control greed that can endanger everyone); and

3) a democracy is what we value. (Not a corporate oligarchy where businesses run the country).

The Best is the Enemy of the Good

Recently, I've been thinking about the expression, "The best is the enemy of the good." Just exactly what does it mean? I think it describes the tendency of some jerks to criticize any new idea that is not perfect. It is like saying, "Sure we are dealing with a crappy situation but your solution isn't perfect, and I don't think we should settle for anything less than perfect."

This allows the jerk to take a position of moral superiority and yet not offer anything of value. I am amazed how often people put up with this. Someone offers a good solution and the jerk takes the opportunity to raise their eyebrow, dip their chin, and say "It's not perfect so I can't agree." Most often we as an audience say "Gee, I guess you may be right."

This is a subtle form of jerkiness, and I think it may hide an inferiority complex. Sometimes we choose a tranquil workplace over dealing with people like this. There is a quote by Bill Lemley who says, "When nobody around you seems to measure up, it's time to check your yardstick." See the web site at www.quotegarden.com/perfection.html.

Each of us must decide to what extent jerk behavior will be tolerated but all of it has a cost.

So High Self-Esteem is a Good Thing, Right?

During a job interview the candidate appears to have high self-confidence and self-esteem, and you're thinking this is going well. But they may be masking something else.

Michael Kernis, Ph.D., Professor of Psychology at the University of Georgia, has done research on this topic and says, "There are many kinds of high self-esteem, and in this study we found that for those in which it is fragile and shallow it's no better than having low self-esteem."

Those who truly have high self-esteem were less likely to be verbally defensive by blaming others or providing excuses when discussing past transgressions or threatening experiences. Those with fragile or shallow self-esteem were more verbally defensive. The professor sums up by saying these findings support the view that high self-esteem involving heightened defensiveness reflects insecurity, fragility, and less-than-optimal functioning rather than a healthy psychological outlook. A summary of his findings is in a 2008 article at www.webmd.com by Jennifer Warner.

My conclusion is that self-esteem can be difficult to interpret and HR professionals should probably stay out of the psychoanalytic business. I think that this is true of pre-employment tests as well. A good pre-employment test should be related to the job environment.

The WAT works not because it is psychoanalytic, but because it looks at attitudes related to social aspects of the workplace. The Test makes the following assumptions:

1) The workplace is a social environment.

2) People should get along with each other.

3) People with bad attitudes don't play well with others.

4) Certain work-related attitudes pre-dispose people to act in certain ways.

5) Workplace attitudes can be measured.

6) Disruptive people, often described as jerks, have problematic workplace attitudes.

7) Jerks, identified by behavior or consensus, are happy to reveal all of their workplace attitudes because they are proud of those attitudes. They will do this on a test, or away from a supervisor, and usually not in a job interview.

Chronic Jerks and Self-Important Jerks

I believe that some people are chronic jerks, that they enjoy their status, and that they are unlikely to change. Sometimes jerk behavior is rewarded and seldom punished. For example, if the boss is a jerk he or she may hire or promote other jerks because they share certain attitudes as well as beliefs and values that form the basis of the attitudes.

Then there is the self-important jerk, a person who is essentially saying "I'm more important than you are." This is expressed in a variety of ways such as making people wait. It seems that some assistants as well as the bosses enjoy the phrase "Mr. Jones (or Ms. Jones) will see you now." This usually occurs after you've been waiting a long period of time. Have you waited more than an hour to see someone? More than two or three hours for a technician to fix something in your home? How long have you waited in a long line for service because supervisors did not want to come out front to help the clerks?

A variation of this phenomenon is "to be fashionably late." Some people are consistently late. They appear never to be on time unless of course they're meeting with someone who is more important than they are.

This game is not only played by executives but can also be played by plumbers, electricians, carpenters and cable installers. I once waited for carpet to be installed five times because they kept canceling the appointment or did not show up. Some people are fortunate enough to be paid by the hour. For the rest of us, we usually just have to put up with these jerks.

Some Thoughts on Jerks and Creativity

The presence of a jerk on a team can stop creativity. This is because creativity usually thrives when there is tolerance, open-mindedness, appreciation of innovation, and willingness to consider multiple possibilities. Creativity requires encouragement. Jerks can stop this process because they demean others and they generally pollute the work environment with caustic remarks.

What are the conditions of creativity? I suggest that creativity requires: persistent determination to solve the problem; willingness to expand the boundaries of the problem; willingness to consider multiple possibilities; and respect for something I call the "gestalt."

The persistent determination to solve the problem is somewhat self-explanatory. It involves a willingness to think about a problem and to learn as much as possible about things related to the problem. In short, it is strong curiosity. It is also a lack of certitude and jerks tend to be blessed by certitude. Bertrand Russell said "The whole problem with the world is that fools and fanatics are always so certain of themselves, and wiser people so full of doubts."

A willingness to expand the boundaries of the problem is another form of open-mindedness. If the problem is faster communication, then breeding faster horses for the pony express is not as good as working on the telegraph. In fact, sometimes creative innovation finds a solution to a problem that you didn't know existed. The Walkman and the iPod come to mind.

Willingness to consider multiple possibilities is a process where ideas need to be evaluated without regard to status or personality. I recall a story of a group of executives trying to solve the problem of long wait times at elevators at a busy hotel. There were many complaints and they finally decided it was necessary to tear out several hotel rooms to make way for more elevators. The lady cleaning the rooms overheard them and muttered that she thought that this was silly. One of the executives was smart enough to ask her why she thought it was silly. She said, "Well at the last place I worked they had the same problem. Then they installed mirrors on each side of the elevators and people were so busy looking at themselves that they forgot about the wait time and the complaints stopped." If the executive was a jerk, I suspect that he would not have asked the advice of the cleaning lady.

Finally, respect for the gestalt. This is a little more difficult to explain but many scientists suggest that oftentimes their pre-occupation with a problem is rewarded with a sudden solution. It springs full-blown into their mind, sometimes in the shower or late at night. These insights must be respected and they seem to be the result of patient open-mindedness. Again, jerks seem to be excluded from this process.

Creative people may seem to be very stubborn in their preoccupation with solving a problem. Some can be loners, and I believe that creative types who also have people skills will find their lives even more conducive to greater creativity. I found an interesting observation in the 2007 book *Blind Spots* by Madeleine L. Van Hecke, Ph.D. She says that creative people are able to live with ambiguity more so than other people.

Maybe you want to make your workplace more creative. In this case you need to encourage all the workers, provide positive feedback when they bring new ideas to you, and be tolerant of different work styles.

Is It Easier to Hire Good Workers During a Recession?

Dare I say the word "Recession?" In the late-1970s, Alfred Kahn who was Jimmy Carter's chief economic advisor used this word in one of his discussions with the press. He was quickly summoned to the White House for a woodshed moment and was told to abandon this negative word. He replaced it with the word banana even singing the song, "Yes we have no bananas, we have no bananas today."

Now assuming that we are in one big banana, how does this affect the hiring process? It would seem that with more people looking for work, good people would be easier to find.

Many job candidates in a time of major economic challenge may be looking for a new position because they are facing serious financial problems, some are facing foreclosure, and some have less than excellent credit reports. A lot of times candidates are automatically disqualified because of their credit rating.

The truth is that many people are in trouble because of circumstances, not irresponsibility.

For example, it could be the housing meltdown, it could be a serious illness in their family, or maybe they started a business that didn't work out as expected. It is better to judge applicants **not** by their credit report but by their work-related attitudes.

Are they entitled versus unassuming?
Are they adversarial versus accommodating?
Are they egocentric versus people oriented?
Are they judgmental versus accepting?
Are they vindictive versus forgiving?
Are they insubordinate versus respectful?
Are they undisciplined versus self-disciplined?

56

Overall, there is not much good about a recession but there are tools to help the interviewer in challenging times. The WAT looks at the attitudes listed above and more.

What's up Down Under?

The Workplace Attitudes Test is also used outside the U.S. and in 2008 I received an e-mail from Fiona Smith, Work Space Editor of the *The Australian Financial Review,* who wanted to interview me about the Workplace Attitudes Test.

We scheduled a call for 4:00 p.m. Washington, D.C. time, two days later. When I got the call I said, "Good morning, you're up early," and she seemed pleased that I knew there was a 17-hour time difference. I try to sound moderately intelligent with reporters and be invariably nice because I remember the quote, "Never argue with a person who buys ink by the barrel."

Fiona Smith was very nice (I hope you read this Fiona) and was writing about some companies in the Australian workplace where jerks and bullies are less tolerated than they used to be. Her article is entitled "Now be nice – there's no place for bullies" and it is in *The Australian Financial Times,* June 17, 2008. She starts her article by saying, "At Arup Australasia, there is a 'no dickheads' policy. If you can't treat others with respect, you won't be tolerated."

She is quoting the managing director of this engineering consulting firm, Robert Care. Robert, I couldn't have said it better myself. The article goes on to cite examples of intolerance for intolerance, or as the fine folks down under might say "We are not going to dick around with dickheads."

Then Fiona went on to describe how to identify these people and she found me -- well, what I mean is she found my WAT. The following four paragraphs are from her article.

"There are many consultancies offering psychological testing to make sure that new recruits will fit into the culture of their new employer, but one company in the U.S. is selling a test specifically targeted at weeding out jerks.

The president of Allegiance Research Group, Dale Paulson, says his Workplace Attitudes Test has not yet been picked up by many big corporations but is proving popular with small businesses, franchises, associations, and even police.

About ninety percent of problems come from ten percent of employees – people who have chips on their shoulders' he says. The 45 question test, developed nine years ago, is very effective at the lower levels of the organization and for supervisors, he says, but, realistically, is unlikely to be used at the top of the organization. 'If you are making ten million dollars you get to be a jerk' he says.

But wouldn't people with a history of difficulty working with others be tempted to lie about their attitudes in a test? 'No, they are actually proud of their attitudes. They come in and say things like, 'it's a dog eat dog world,' 'you can't trust anyone,' and, 'if you step on my toes and you don't apologize you are going to get broken toes.' he says."

And so folks, I'm here to tell you that in addition to shrimp on the barbie and Foster's beer, there are jerks in Australia, except they are generally referred to as "dickheads."

The Greatest Generation, Baby-Boomers, Gen X, Y and Me

There is an interesting and possibly apocryphal story concerning Pompeii, the Italian city that was buried during a catastrophic eruption of the volcano of Mount Vesuvius in 79 AD. It is reported that graffiti on a bathhouse wall said, "What is happening to the younger generation?" Whether this story is true or not, every generation seems puzzled and bemused by subsequent generations.

Newer generations are equally critical of the previous generation. This reminds me of the old saying, "The grandson wants to remember what the son wants to forget." Suffice it to say, generations are different and they approach life and work differently.

Tom Brokaw, the TV anchor, wrote books about the "Greatest Generation." This is the generation that grew up during the 1930's Depression, won World War II, developed the suburbs, and spawned the "Baby-Boomer" generation. Mr. Brokaw drew so much attention to that generation and did so many interviews that one wag was inspired to quip, "The Greatest Generation has just delivered a cease-and-desist order against Tom Brokaw!"

Now it is the Baby-Boomer generation that is beginning to retire from the workplace and is gradually being replaced by Gen X, Gen Y, and Gen Me. It is these generations that are receiving much attention from HR experts.

Definitions and terms vary but they roughly go like this:

Gen X was born from 1965 to about 1980.

Gen Y was born from 1980 to about 1995.

Gen Me tends to be a more pejorative term and overlaps Gen X and Gen Y, and they were born after 1970.

Another term that is often used to describe a generation is millennials and it tends to be another name for Gen Y.

I recently had the opportunity to see the noted author and speaker, Dave Caperton. His book is *Happiness is a Funny Thing* and after his speech, I introduced myself and eventually we talked about workplace attitudes. He later sent me a very perceptive e-mail that said:

"Civility seems to be an endangered species and workplaces are also struggling with more diversity of cultures which certainly causes misunderstanding and conflict. Add to that the generational differences - - particularly electronic media and conversation - - that have rendered millennials less skilled at face-to-face communication especially when it crosses age and power boundaries. A lot of younger people seem overly casual or don't seem to even observe many social boundaries that once defined the workplace hierarchy as well as the treatment of customers."

In an article entitled "Generation Y: They've Arrived at Work With a New Attitude" appearing in *USA Today* in 2005, columnist Stephanie Armour describes a 22 year old young lady in flip-flops at her desk listening to her iPod and saying that she doesn't want work to be her life. She says:

"This is Generation Y, a force of as many as 70 million, and the first wave now embarking on their careers, taking their place in an increasingly multigenerational workplace."

She quotes Bruce Tulgan of Rainmaking Thinking, who co-authored *Managing Generation Y* with Carolyn Martin, as describing Gen Y as "having been pampered, nurtured and programmed with a slew of activities since they were toddlers meaning they are both high performance and high maintenance." He continues, "If you thought you saw a clash when Generation X came into the workplace, that was a fake punch. The haymaker is coming now."

Jean M. Twenge, Ph.D., wrote a book in 2006 whose title seems to say it all, *Generation Me: Why Today's Young Americans Are More Confident, Assertive, Entitled -- and More Miserable Than Ever Before.*" (Would I be too cynical to ask if they are going to make the rest of us miserable isn't it only fair that they're a little miserable themselves?)

She says, "Instead of creating well-adjusted, happy children, the self-esteem movement has created an army of little narcissists. Narcissism is a very negative personality trait linked to aggression and poor relations with others."

Oh boy. Here are a few more.

Mike Kraus, offers strategies to retail store managers who are faced with the statement, "Pay me more or I'm quitting." And Rebecca Mazin authored an article called "How Many Employees Will Have the Flu on Monday?" This refers to likely absences after the Super Bowl. She suggests that employers track absences after weekends and three-day holidays. These articles are on the web site www.allbusiness.com.

In the 2007 Junior Achievement/Deloitte Teen Ethics Survey, about forty percent of the teenagers surveyed believed that lying, cheating, plagiarizing, and violence are sometimes necessary to succeed in school. The results are on the web site www.deloitte.com.

Well which is it? Is that graffiti on the Pompeii wall accurate in that older generations will always disparage younger generations, or are Gen X, Gen Y, and Gen Me really going to hell in a hand basket?

Referring back to Aristotle's Golden Mean, I think that the answer is a decisive yes and no. The point is that all generational labels are generalities. They are useful if they are correct more than fifty percent of the time. The problem that I am concerned with is whether the next person I hire will be disruptive in the work place. Who is to say which generation has the most jerks or turkeys? Therefore, I recommend that you assess everyone as an individual. It is important to keep in mind that you are hiring a person, not a generation.

WAT does not ask for any demographic information such as gender or age. It is kept as blind as possible, so we do not have information about generations. For clients who want more in-depth analysis there is a place at the end of the test for a code, and they instruct the job applicant to enter a code in that space. They can use it to identify things like specific job title or city which enables them to bundle test results together and see trends or parameters, or to identify a range of attitude measurements that best fits a specific job title.

Believe It or Not, Jerks Have Their Defenders

In a world that claims that there are no absolutes, believe me, there are some absolutes. Newtonian physics is not cancelled out by Einstein's theory of relativity, especially if you hit a tree at one hundred miles an hour in your car.

Why do I bring this up? Well, I've been reading some blogs lately that say one jerk in the workplace may be a good thing. The arguments go like this: some people are indispensable even if they are jerks; it is impossible to find enough reasonable people; and one jerk can help keep everyone else on their toes.

Dr. Robert Sutton's book, *The No-Asshole Rule: Building a Civilized Workplace and Surviving One That Isn't*, points out that there is a calculated "total cost of assholes" and it is surprisingly high, plus it is almost impossible to enforce a civility rule with one asshole (or jerk) in the workplace. It goes on to describe how jerks are personally abusive and that they tend to treat subordinates with derision and superiors with some respect.

Mark I. Schickman, an employment law attorney, in his review of the aforementioned book, says that jerks "take credit for other people's work. They manage expectations by making employees feel bad about themselves. They have the laser-like ability to find the weakest, most insecure people and focus their aggression on them. The symptomatic behaviors include insults, threats, teasing, shaming and ostracizing." He also talks about companies that have civility codes. This article can be found at the web site www.hrheroblogs.com/resources/2008/02/06.

Recently, I started a discussion session on the HR web site called ERE and the address is http://ere.net/forum. The topic was "Should HR Be Pro-Actively Anti Jerk?" I even cited the book, *The No Asshole Rule: Building a Civilized Workplace and Surviving One That Isn't*. About eighty percent of the comments tended to agree that jerks are costly and that HR should do its part to bring tranquility to the workplace. However, about twenty percent of the comments demonstrated a fair amount of tolerance for jerks.

One comment asked (in Latin), who is going to watch the watchers? My Latin is non-existent so to add insult to injury I had to look up the quote on Wikipedia. Another person said that "One man's victim is another man's whiner." Someone else said "The purpose of HR is to serve as a protective device. Make sure everything is legal, fair, and compliant and quash anything likely to result in litigation. When you are done with all that then by all means, you may devote a few minutes per day to your Utopian ideals on human potential."

Others suggested that jerks are necessary to shake things up and to keep people on their toes, and that if someone is really good at their job then jerkiness should be tolerated.

There you have it, some justifications for tolerating jerks in the workplace: (1) who has the right to judge? (2) the victims may just be whiners; (3) the anti-jerk idea is utopian; (4) people need jerks to motivate them; and (5) some jerks are so important that we need to tolerate them.

This is an old debate. There are times when certain actions should be taken to guard against the worst instincts of some people. Even gun-rights advocates tend to agree that hand-grenades and bazookas should be regulated. I'll grant that some people would disagree, but they are jerks.

Recommendations if You Have to Deal With a Jerk

It is not enough to get a job, it is also important to keep a job. As mentioned earlier, people tend to be hired for aptitude and fired for attitude. This section describes strategies and skills that are analogous to those of a bomb-diffusion expert.

After reading many articles, I find that a lot of management consultants have an overly optimistic view of how to deal with a jerk. This is particularly true when they give advice about dealing with boss jerks. They tend to tell you to express yourself and confront the jerk and, if possible, to limit your interaction.

Other experts are pessimistic and suggest that you can't out-jerk a jerk and that you can't out-scream a screamer. Jerks are jerks precisely because they are so difficult to deal with.

Both views contain some good advice but not much detail is provided. In this section I will endeavor to provide specific recommendations.

Confrontation

The general advice here is to calmly, privately, and briefly confront the jerk and avoid further interaction if possible. Good luck! Calmly, privately and briefly may work but avoiding further interaction is problematic.

Let's look at the case of the insidious back-stabber who is a co-worker. Basically the backstabber is someone who is nice to you to your face but sabotages you with others. This is an instance where confrontation may be advisable.

After you make up your mind that you will not tolerate this type of behavior, you can say something like this, "You presented my idea as your own. Please don't do that again."

Or you can say, "Do not blame me for you missing your deadline."

Or "Why am I excluded from the next planning session?"

The above examples require calmness because oftentimes we exacerbate problems when we respond emotionally. In the best-case scenario you will have time to think about the situation and prepare what you will say

But what if you are surprised by a jerk? There are some tricks to recapture your composure and/or to turn things in your favor and here are some examples.

* When a jerk surprises you, gain a few seconds to calm yourself down by asking for clarification.

* When responding to a jerk, use the words, "I feel" or "I believe" because no one can argue with how we feel or believe.

* Try a re-frame where you say something like, "I see this as an opportunity, not a problem" or "The client is going through a difficult time and we should not take his curtness personally."

If you are not comfortable confronting a co-worker directly, you can go to the supervisor, and finally to the HR Department. Researchers have found that most people do *not* confront jerks. The corporate training company VitalSmarts surveyed 900 people about their thoughts on "untouchable employees" defined as poor-performing, rude, and/or obnoxious co-workers. About three-quarters of the respondents said that they avoid confronting these people, choosing instead to complain to co-workers or to try and work around them. My guess is that this is due to fear of retaliation or not knowing how to confront effectively.

Set Priorities

As a research consultant, I had the opportunity to work with the CEO of a large cable company. This individual was very busy and valued my input. The problem was that he made unreasonable demands and would become irritated. If a project normally took two weeks, he asked for the results after one week.

What to do? I came up with a system that solved the problem. I simply asked him to grade his request. This is like the grading system used in schools. For example if something needed to be done immediately or in the near future it would receive a grade of A. If something could be put off it might receive a grade of C. After I received instructions, I simply confirmed what is important and proceeded to work on the A list first. This solved the problem and we had a long and productive relationship.

Reinforce the Positive

Everyone likes positive feedback. Here is how I used it to solve a problem when I was teaching at a University. I prided myself with having an open-door policy where students could drop in whenever they wanted to discuss things. Not surprisingly, I spent a lot of time discussing their problems. There was no end of problems and very few solutions.

Then I decided to make a sign and post it over my desk. It read "I do not discuss problems, but I am happy to discuss alternative solutions." After that when a student came in and said "I have a problem I want to discuss," I would simply point to the sign over my head. What a difference! The office visits were cut in half and students actually came in with positive ideas.

Separate the Person from the Problem

Are human beings rational creatures with emotions? I believe that human beings are better described as emotional beings who are secondarily rational. In other words, I believe that most people act first and justify later. This puts us in a rather unfortunate situation. A little like fire, shoot, aim! I wish that human behavior was more like aim, then stop and think. But often it is not.

Look for patterns of behavior. Look for times when people are what I call on "cruise-control" By that, I mean they get emotional about certain things no matter what. It is a knee-jerk reaction and it is predictable. Do yourself a favor and try to avoid these situations by taking pre-emptive action.

For example, if your boss goes ballistic when the office runs out of dairy creamer -- do yourself a favor and go out and buy some. I'm always amazed when a restaurant located right next to a grocery store doesn't have sugar or some other basic commodity like napkins. Hey, they can take a buck or two and go buy some sugar or napkins.

Non-Certitude Strategies

Phrases such as "I know I'm right and you're wrong" tend to rub people the wrong way. Conversely, if you start a phrase with "I'm not sure, but I think this is right," then people are more likely to believe you and be cooperative.

Einstein is reputed to have said to a dinner companion, who complimented him on one of his theories, that "all the facts in the world will not prove me absolutely right, but one little insignificant fact can prove me wrong." It is this type of attitude that seems to endear us to people. It is a subliminal acknowledgment that you could be wrong and they could be right.

Sometimes a little humor helps to defuse a tense situation. But this works better between co-workers, rather than employee to supervisor.

Did you know that according to the law if you use phrases like "I believe" or "I think" or "It seems to me" that it is very unlikely that you will be sued for libel? Under the law you have a right to your beliefs. But you do not have the right to say something is true when you know it is not. For example you can be sued if you tell people that your boss or co-worker is mentally ill when you know they are not and have no proof. In other words, you are simply saying it because you are mad at them and want to ruin their reputation.

The Cost of Being Right

"This is a better way to do it."
"No it's not, my way is better and I can prove it. I told you I was right!"

And so it goes. Oftentimes, when you wear the other person down, you get to be right. But what have you won? You don't get a trophy, you don't get a certificate, and you probably haven't changed the other person's mind because now they are very angry at you. If you put a dollar value on being right, it is probably very similar to that phrase "Do you want my two cents worth?" The price seems to be accurate. Just a thought.

A Buddhist Parable

The Buddhist religion feels so strongly about prohibiting certitude that there is a famous parable about it.

It seems that there was an impoverished farmer whose son had the good fortune of capturing a wild horse. This would increase the farmer's fortune considerably and when his neighbors heard the story they came to him and said "how wonderful and how lucky you are." And the farmer replied, "Perhaps."

Then one day the horse broke loose and ran away. The farmer's neighbors said "How sad, how unlucky you are." The farmer replied, "Perhaps."

But then the horse returned, and with a mate. The farmer now had two horses and was again congratulated only to reply, "Perhaps."

When the farmer's son tried to ride the horse he was thrown off and broke his leg. Neighbors again said he was unlucky and the farmer said "Perhaps."

Then the rulers of the community came to the farm to recruit the son into the Army. But the son could not go as he had a broken leg. When neighbors mentioned that this was good fortune, the farmer replied "Perhaps."

Well you get the idea. Certitude does not rank high among Buddhists and you may want to consider it as a workplace strategy. A more mellow attitude may get you more than you think.

The Über Apology

Sometimes, we all make mistakes. Über or ueber from the German translates to over, above, meta, and super. Here I define it as a super apology. Basically it means that if you beat yourself up, enough people generally will come to your defense. It can even turn around a person known to be very strict, like your supervisor. Let me illustrate with the following dialog.

Assume that this conversation is going on between you and your supervisor. As you apologize more and more, the supervisor begins to soften.

Me: "I'm sorry I made a mistake."
Supervisor: "You certainly did and it is unacceptable."

Me: "I don't know how I could have done it. I feel just terrible, just terrible."
Supervisor: "Well it's unfortunate."

Me: "It's probably one of the dumbest things I have ever done. I should not have done it. I should have thought more carefully. If only I had been better prepared."
Supervisor: "Well it's not really that bad."

Me: "No, no, it's terrible. I really screwed up. You probably have never done anything this bad."
Supervisor: "Oh I wouldn't say that."
Me: "No, no I am totally to blame, I should be ashamed. I am ashamed."

You can go on like this until you both get tired of it. Usually your accuser will start to defend you. And you can play it out until you think the game should end. If you don't you use it too often, it can be quite effective and it tends to put things in perspective which is good.

The Role-Reversal Apology

This is where you say "It's my fault and I know I put you in a bad situation." You may have to say it more than one time. What you are doing here is implying that you understand that what you did has repercussions for the other person.

The more you show that you understand how difficult you made it for the other person, the more the focus changes away from you. The conversation with your boss might go like this.

The boss: "How could you do such a stupid thing?"
Me: "I know, it wasn't good. I suppose I put you in a very bad situation."

The boss: "Yes I had to explain it to my boss."
Me: "It must be difficult for someone when they are put in a bad situation like you were."

The boss: "Well it's not good but I was able to handle it."
Me: "I will try never to put you in that situation again."

The boss: "I appreciate that."
Me: "Thank you" followed by a graceful exit.

The above example shows how you can take the attention away from your mistake. It also shows that you are concerned with how your work reflects on your boss. Win-win.

Defusing Phrases

Defusing phrases are things you can say that help others to calm down. It sometimes makes a difference if you show empathy to a person who is behaving like a jerk and try to see the situation from their point of view or find a grain of truth in some things they are saying.

Here are some examples:

"You make a good point."
"Now I understand."
"I never looked at it that way before."
"You have really helped me with that."
"Even though we have disagreements sometimes, we can still work toward the common goal of this organization."

There are a lot of variations on this theme. The point is to acknowledge the other person in some way. Oftentimes, the goal of another person, even if they are angry, is to be understood. Do it.

Irrational Phrases

Sometimes it helps to use phrases that seem to be irrational but have a good feeling. For example, "If I were you, I would feel the same way." This is one of the dumbest things I have ever heard. I don't know what it is but, strangely, I like to hear it. It makes me feel that the other person is in my corner and they have my concerns at heart. I do not take them literally. Of course if they were me they would feel the same way! Duh.

Bill Clinton, a master communicator, understood this concept when he said "I feel your pain." Really, Bill. It does make me feel better. Of course, it doesn't mean anything but it works.

Phrases That Jerks Use Before They Insult You

Here are some phrases that jerks may say before they insult you.

"Let me be brutally honest"
"I know that I shouldn't say this but . . ."
"I'm not sure but haven't you gained a little weight?"

The point is you may want to cut them off at the pass. If the person says "Let me brutally honest," you might want to cut them off by saying, "No, I prefer your usual dishonesty." Sometimes humor helps in awkward situations.

Office Proselytes

From time to time, you may run into people at work who out of righteous zeal or concern for your immortal soul, want to convert you to their religion. I sort of know because my dissertation chairman was a Mormon and he invited me to some "meetings." For me it didn't take, but I rather like Mormons especially after I learned that they may be the only organization that would welcome you into their bomb shelter in time of need.

One of my close relatives is a Jehovah's Witness and I can tell you about people who are trying to convert you. Now that is a persistent group! My relative actually had some Jehovah Witnesses see me when I was visiting Mexico, but usually she sends them to my home. It took years to convince her that I'm probably a lost cause.

My religion you ask? I tend to be a follower of Ben Franklin. I particularly like his prayer that goes something like this: "Lord show me the way to be kind to my fellow man for that is the best way that I can worship you." I admit that I'm a little light on certitude and relate to Mark Twain who is reputed to have said "It pains me to think of countless generations of native Hawaiians who, before the arrival of missionaries, were ignorant of eternal damnation."

Still, I have a lot of patience for people who are trying to convert me. After all, they are concerned about my welfare and when they come to my house, if they are Jehovah Witnesses or Mormons, they won't drink my booze, smoke my cigars or drink my coffee.

Albeit, trying to convert someone at work is not a good idea and if it persists, it falls under the category of jerk behavior and should not be tolerated. This goes for anti-religious rants as well. (I discuss this next under the heading "Some Thoughts on Religious

Tolerance.")

To sum up, I handle proselyte approaches much like a situation I once faced in Las Vegas. I was there to give a speech and my wife was not with me. I decide to take a walk when a very attractive lady of the night followed me for two blocks. From her standpoint it was a matter of youth and beauty meets forlorn and desperate.

I think of that old Karl Malden credit card ad when he says, "If you lose your card what are you *going to do?* What are you *going to do*?" When the young lady finally approached, I said to her, "Young lady, you're not wasting my time, but I'm sure as hell wasting yours." Polite but persistent. (Did I mention that my wife is my editor?) So what are you going to do about proselytizing? Make it clear that religious discussions don't belong in the workplace but be polite and persistent about it.

Some Thoughts on Religious Tolerance

Bill Maher stars in HBO's *Real Time* and he brings us the movie "Religulous." I like Bill Maher and think he's the best ambassador for the blue states. He is half Jewish and half Catholic and his early quips about the confessional are hilarious, "Bless me father for I have sinned. I think you have met my lawyer, Mr. Cohen."

I am sure that he regards the Catholic Church as the First Church of the Perpetual Second Chance, Mormons as purveyors of bullet-proof underwear, Protestants as snake charmers, and other forms of religion as delusional. Bill, in the name of rationality, you are a bit extreme and this is why I did not like your movie *Religulous*. Too many straw men and it seemed too easy.

Senator Goldwater, when running for President, said, "Extremism in the defense of liberty is no vice." Bill, I am sure you are pure of heart but I say that "extremism in the defense of doubt" is a vice because it is another form of intolerance.

I admit I may have my doubts about the talking snake, Jonah and the whale, and Noah and the flood. In fact I may best be described as an agnostic with foxhole reservations (there are no agnostics in foxholes). Still I don't think that agnosticism and certitude, even about doubt, make a good platform. It's like saying I am not sure about these things, and you can't be sure about your religion so you're wrong.

Shoot down the zealots to your heart's content but give a little credit to Mother Theresa, Mahatma Gandhi, and Albert Schweitzer. You can call them self-deluded do-gooders but they still did a lot of good. P.S. Bill, I still like you.

Summarizing Strategies for Dealing With Jerks

There you have it, some techniques that can be used to defuse jerk-created situations. You should de-personalize, be non-emotional, avoid certitude, think in terms of "perhaps," show some empathy, and understand that oftentimes it's a game. If none of these things help, keep good notes and think about requesting a transfer.

Hire For Attitude, Train Later

Some companies do hire by looking at attitude and figure they can then train the person to do the job. A great example comes from Southwest Airlines and is described by Keith Harrell in his 2004 book, *Attitude is Everything*. He says:

"Southwest recruiter Jose Colmenares told *Fast Company* magazine that he didn't look for a fixed set of skills or experiences when hiring flight attendants. Instead, he searched for what the magazine described as 'the perfect blend of energy, humor, team spirit, and self confidence to match Southwest's famously offbeat and customer-obsessed culture."

Unlike other airlines, this airline has done well through the years in good economies and bad and possibly it is the attitudes of their employees that make the difference.

Now, another airline story. I remember when airlines were

concerned about your comfort. The friendly flight attendants really wanted to know what you preferred. Today, when the overhead luggage rack looks commodious and you find your knees in close proximity to your nose, those days seem long gone. Nowadays the flight crews, working under stress, have more important things to do.

But back in the day, airline executives were more concerned about service. I remember reading an article about a major airline finding that most of their complaints were directed at ten percent of their personnel and they actually wanted to know why. The reason I am relating this is that their solution was very clever and was another one of the inspirations that lead me to develop the Workplace Attitudes Test that screens for bad attitudes.

Their pre-employment interviews clearly did not work and turkeys were getting through. I define a turkey as someone with bad workplace attitudes. For example you do not want a flight attendant who says with a frown, "Would you like coffee, tea or milk . . . whatever?"

The airline needed a system to weed out the turkeys. Like the Workplace Attitudes Test, they wanted to identify bad attitudes in potential flight attendants and I think that their solution borders on genius.

They had each prospect go to the podium and talk about their hobbies, their pets, and their aspirations. Each could go on for as long as they wanted and it oftentimes was up to twenty minutes. The presentations were not videotaped. *Instead, the camera was focused on the audience.*

The goal was not to evaluate the presenters but to evaluate how tolerant or patient each member of the audience happened to be. Some were doing their nails, frowning, or talking to colleagues. Others showed great patience and respect. Guess which ones got the job? And guess what happened to the number of complaints.

Another word for this type of observation by social scientists is called unobtrusive measures and a book by this name was one of my favorites in grad school. There are many creative ways that you can test a person's attitudes. For example, if you are looking for those who are people-oriented and have empathy, try setting up a little test as they walk into the building for an interview. The following example is paraphrased from the 2007 book, *Blind Spots*.

In a classic study conducted at the Princeton Theological Seminary decades ago, ministry students were led to believe that they needed to rush over to another building in order to deliver a sermon they had been in the midst of preparing. The topic was being a Good Samaritan. In this study each student was routed through a doorway in which an accomplice of the researcher was slumped and apparently ill. Of those who believed they were late, only one in ten offered help!

Identifying Jerks with De-Merits

This book talks about identifying people who may be jerks in the workplace. It is based on my views and research, but what about the views of others such as society as a whole or people who work with a jerk?

How about the libertarian argument that we shouldn't regulate behavior? Well we do regulate behavior. Duels such as the one between Aaron Burr and Alexander Hamilton are quite effectively banned these days. Also, there are very few gun fights like in the old west. We re-framed the issue and said that consensual duels and six-gun face-offs are not self-defense or a matter of honor. We decided to call it murder. Societies are formed for the benefit of the people and laws are passed by their representatives to enhance their education, health, safety, and even happiness as stated in the U.S. Declaration of Independence.

How about people in the workplace defining jerk behavior? I suggest a humorous approach -- anonymous jerk de-merits!

For example, give every employee 100 anonymous de-merit points each month to spend on anyone who has acted like a jerk. Each employee would make a list of people that they interact with and they could assign de-merits in any amount to anyone on that list. Totals would come in at the end of each month.

Should the cumulative list be public? I'm not sure. Should you take action against those who get consistently high scores? Good question. All I'm saying here is that it is possible to define jerk behavior and it is possible to identify it. It is best not to hire jerks in the first place, but if you already have them in the workplace you need to decide what you can do about it.

Guesstimating the Cost of Hiring a Jerk

I believe that the vast majority of your problems usually come from a small percent of your workers, probably 5% or less. Therefore, it's really important to know how much a jerk can cost you. Well, for a blue-collar worker it costs about $16,028, for a professional or white-color worker it costs about $70,312, and for a salesperson it costs about $56,200.

Wouldn't it be nice if we could be so precise? The truth is, I cannot tell you exactly how much it costs to hire a jerk! But I can tell you it's a lot.

I own a small business and the jerks that I hired have cost me in excess of six figures. Fortunately, they were hired as independent contractors rather than regular employees (so I could easily terminate them) but the resulting and lasting damage of jerks does not respect these boundaries. It is another reason I decided to do research in this area.

Figuring Lifetime Value of Lost Business

In a 2007 article featured in the *McKinsey Quarterly* there is something called "TCJ" which means Total Cost of Jerks. This includes some very difficult-to-quantify concepts such as greater turnover, lower productivity, absenteeism and even higher rates of disability and stress-related illnesses. This doesn't even mention lawsuits. All this can often be attributable to jerks.

This brings us back to the question, how much does a jerk cost? Again the answer is "a lot" but this is not a very satisfactory answer. Allow me to add one more concept which may provide a little more precision -- it is the lifetime value of a customer or client. You can estimate this for yourself but here are some real-life examples.

The Cost of Teaching Someone a Lesson

I felt sorry for one individual who was having trouble finding a job and I decided to give this person the opportunity to do some focus groups with me. I mean I would be right there in the room, what could possibly go wrong?

We were working with one of my best clients, an education association. In the course of doing a focus group with the staff this individual commented that the people in the room appeared to be extremely "conservative." Well, these educators did not like to be described as conservative. I tried to calm things down but he seemed to think he had an important point to make and would not stop.

He thought he was teaching them a lesson and he was on a power trip! Goodbye client. The previous three years this association had paid my company about $40,000 a year. After that incident they never used my company again. How much did this cost me? Who knows the specific figure, but it was a lot.

The Cost of Insulting Someone

You may be familiar with the great rivalry between Ferrari and Lamborghini. These two exotic car companies have been fighting over a very limited market for years. Not that I'd know, since I drive a Toyota Camry!

First, there was the Ferrari. Many years ago Ferruccio Lamborghini, a tractor manufacturing magnate, was having mechanical problems with his Ferrari and when he went to talk to Enzo Ferrari about the problem and possible solutions, he was given the brush off. After all, why should Enzo take advice from a tractor manufacturer? It is well known that Enzo could be a bit of a jerk.

Ferruccio stormed off vowing to build a better car and he created the Lamborghini. How much did this cost Enzo? I'm not certain, but probably millions of dollars. There would probably be a lot more Ferraris on the road had Enzo been less of a jerk. (From *Automobile Magazine* at www.automobilemag.com)

The Cost of Ignoring Someone

I already told you about the loss of a major client and this was a big hit for my company. But you don't have to lose many thousands of dollars to feel the impact. The lifetime value of a client or customer varies according to what type of client or customer they are.

Clients or customers can be occasional large purchasers or repeat small purchasers. I remember the time when I was turning in a car from a lease. I was thinking of purchasing a similar car on a new lease. The salesman, knowing I was there to turn in the previous car, did not have time for me and that is how I changed from being a Volkswagen GTI leaser to a Toyota Camry purchaser.

I've never been back to that dealership. How much has it cost the dealership? Good question. I figure I have not purchased three more cars from them. If they make a profit of $1,500 on each car, then this totals a loss to them of $4,500 plus the lost profit from any related repair business.

The Cost of Making an Unreasonable Request

How about small repeat business? I used to go to a small coffee shop once a day to order a cappuccino. When they were having business problems (which I was not aware of) the owner suggested I was using too many packets of sugar. Since I only used two small packets of sugar, this surprised me. Another customer spoke up and told the owner that she was being foolish and the two began to argue. Although this had a certain entertainment value, I decided never to return to the shop.

How much did that extra packet of sugar cost the owner? Well, I average five cappuccinos a week and I had been going there for about a year. At three bucks a shot, that is $15 a week. When you multiple $15 by 50 weeks, that is $750 lost per year. On the other hand, the proprietor saves a little on sugar.

Overall, I'm afraid you cannot put a precise price on jerk behavior. Be assured, however, that you can't afford one.

A Jerk Can Take $100,000 Out of Your Pocket

I know a businessman whom I will call Jim. He invented a product and got it protected with registered trademarks. He had success with this product but this success lead to a big problem. Another company became jealous and wanted to sell the product even though they did not own it. Well, that company devised a way to tempt Jim to make a deal where they were reps. Then they misrepresented themselves to others and started selling the product and making money. But they never reported this information or paid a percent, as they were required to do, to Jim. Eventually, Jim found out and confronted them about it.

The two owners of that company were extreme jerks and very adversarial and entitled. They refused to give up the product and had a plan that they then put into action: threaten Jim with a lawsuit in a federal courthouse that is over 1,000 miles away; figure that he would never show up in court; and then they would win by default and could continue selling the product. If he did show up in court, they figured he would just last a month or two because of the tremendous cost and stress, and he would drop out -- so again they would win.

Long story short, Jim surprised them and showed up in court. It cost him $100,000! Yes, he paid $10,000 per month to his attorneys for ten months. Finally, just before the trial date, the jerks decided to call it quits because they ran out of money.

It cost $100,000 just to defend against a jerk and just to be able to continue selling a product you own. The judge determined on the first day of the case that Jim owned the product but the lawsuit game had to be played through or Jim could have lost his livelihood. Later, Jim found out that these jerks had done this before to other companies. This is a true story and it almost takes your breath away.

The Traditional Approach to Employee Selection

In some ways the job interview is a little like courtship. That is, people tend to be on their best behavior. I'm reminded of a bumper sticker that I saw when I was in South Carolina. It read, "When I Married Mr. Right, I Had No Idea His First Name Was Always."

In addition to saying something about some married men, this also says a lot about the job interview.

What is the purpose of the job interview? The interviewer wants to know if the prospect is right for the job. The company wants expertise, time, and devotion. The prospect wants opportunity, money, and benefits. The interviewer hopes to ask the right questions and the prospect hopes to give the right answers.

Here is a humorous take on the job interview. Saturday Night Live had a great routine called "Subliminal Man." In a clear stentorian voice he stated what was expected, then in a whisper he said what he really thought. Wouldn't it be nice if this is the way job interviews worked?

Let's see how Subliminal Man does in a typical interview. Our optimistic job candidate, with beer gut, has been somewhat happily unemployed for the past two years. His presence at this interview can best be explained by the insistence of his wife who works fulltime and has recurring backaches from sleeping on the couch.

The Interview with Subliminal Man

Good morning Mr. Johnson.
It's Johnston.
Oh, sorry, Mr. Johnston.
Oh no problem, it happens all the time. (Subliminal Man kicks in: "What a twit")

What attracted you to our company, Mr. Johnston?

I saw your ad in the newspaper. (Subliminal Man: "Actually my wife cut out your ad and put it on my tackle box.")

How much experience have you had driving a semi with a triplex transmission?

Five years, yeah it was five years. Now that I think about it, it could have been six. (Subliminal Man: "None whatsoever, what the hell is a triplex?")

Did you enjoy over-the-road driving?

You bet, ten-four back at you.

You obviously know your way around trucking.

Thanks (Subliminal Man: "Yeah, my kid has a little red one, what a dork.")

What are your salary requirements?

I understand that this type of job pays around $45,000 per year. (Subliminal Man: "Three paychecks and I got that bass boat sweetie.")

Do you see this as a long-term commitment?

Absolutely (Subliminal Man: "At least until duck season!")

Do you have any questions for me?

When would I start if I got the job? (Subliminal Man: "What are you doing Saturday night? My wife will be working.")

We should be making a decision within two weeks.

Thank you, I look forward to hearing from you. (Subliminal Man: "Great, two more weeks on the couch, take your time you wine-sipping twit.")

As you may have guessed, the job interview is somewhat of an inexact science even with the most experienced HR people. This is why several tools should be used.

Background Checks and Recommendations

What can I say about background checks and recommendations? Well, background checks are a necessary evil, and recommendations may not be very effective. You have to do them but you should recognize their limitations.

Background checks take time and money and it is difficult to check everything. They can also be considered an invasion of privacy.

Once a person has signed a consent form you can usually get information from a variety of sources. For example:

Driving records
Vehicle registration
Credit reports
Criminal records
Social Security Number
Education records
Court records
Workers compensation records
Bankruptcy records
Neighbor interviews
Medical records
Property ownership records
Military records
State licensing records
Drug test records
Past employers
Incarceration records
Sex offender lists

The question that I have for you is, "How much time and money do you have?" And, what happens if you already have a jerk at work?

Recommendations do not take time and money but can you trust them? Some former employers are afraid of giving less-than-excellent recommendations because they fear lawsuits. Jerks are skilled at getting recommendations (maybe through intimidation) and are good at covering their tracks. Some jerks also use pity and ask friends to write recommendations and lie for them by saying they did some work for that person. Instead of buyer beware, it is interviewer beware.

They have always been unreliable. In most states, job applicants have the right to read the letters of recommendation and can even file a lawsuit against the writer if the comments are negative. A web site called www.basicjokes.com suggests that the writer use *double entendre* as a strategy. Here are some examples.

To describe the extremely lazy you might say:

"In my opinion you will be very fortunate to get this person to work for you."

Describing the totally inept you might say:

"I enthusiastically recommend this candidate with no qualifications whatsoever."

Other examples include:

"I am pleased to say that this candidate is a former colleague of mine."

"I can assure you that no person would be better for the job."

"I would urge you to waste no time in making this candidate an offer of employment."

I'll bet you won't look at letters of recommendation the same ever again!

Technological Advances are Everywhere

Well, it was bound to happen. There are now web sites designed to create good recommendations and a positive job history. And it wasn't enough to be able to purchase term papers and dissertations, now you can skip all that and buy a degree online. According to Jeff Wizceb, a vice president of HR plus, a division of Allied Barton security services, there are new web sites where you can sign up and create your own work history or fill in gaps in your work history. They provide a company name and address, references, position, salary, etc. One such site is www.careerexcuse.com. Another site offers landlord references and doctor's notes.

Did I mention that I have a Doctorate in astrophysics from MIT? That is the Mudwonk Institute of Technology. If you buy that I'll give you a star!

A Revolutionary Approach to Employee Selection

What is a Good Employee?

If you are looking for good employees why not look for people with good attitudes? The simple answer is--it tends not to work. Looking for good attitudes does not identify individuals with bad attitudes.

The Workplace Attitudes Test (WAT) is designed to screen out people who have a propensity to be disruptive in the workplace. I refer to these people as "turkeys" or "jerks." They are disruptive all out of proportion to their numbers. The assumption underlying the WAT is if you avoid hiring problem employees you will ipso facto hire good employees.

But we can turn this upside down and ask what constitutes a good employee? You say you demand a better definition than "A good employee is someone who is not a bad employee." Well, I'll take a shot.

A good employee is one who is not disruptive. You say you want something more proactive? How about this, a good employee is a person who is slow to judge, who sees the world in gray rather than black and white, and has genuine concern for one's fellow man. In sum, a good employee is a person who is decidedly disinclined to say, "I am doing this for your own good."

So, What Are We Not Looking For?

The WAT measures nine attitudes on a continuum of low to high. Some of these attitudes, when they measure high on the test, are a potential problem for all types of work environments. These attitudes are *judgmental, vindictive, adversarial, egocentric, entitled*, and *insubordinate.*

Then there are three attitudes that may or may not be a potential problem and it depends on the type of organization. These include **risk-inclined, non-traditional**, and **undisciplined.**

An organization with strict hierarchy such as a large bank or a factory wants applicants who are low on risk-inclined and non-traditional. An organization such as a high-tech start-up company may want applicants who are moderate to high on risk-inclined and non-traditional because they reward new ideas.

Undisciplined individuals may be ok in an organization with strict hierarchy if the supervisor keeps careful oversight and enforces clearly-understood rules. Conversely, an informal organization that relies on teamwork or has people working at home requires employees who are self-disciplined because they often work under conditions of limited oversight.

Organizations that rely on creativity are in somewhat of a gray area. An artist or a writer cannot always produce on demand and may flourish when discipline, such as specific work hours, is not imposed on them. Some artists and writers are self-employed and I have heard many famous writers say in interviews that they impose a work schedule on themselves, such as writing four hours every morning, whether their writing is really good that day or not.

Here is a discussion of the nine attitudes that can destroy a workplace.

Judgmental

This is an attitude that can be a problem for any type of work environment and problems can arise from those who score high on judgmental. They feel very defensive, want rules to be strictly enforced with no discretion, and feel compelled to intervene if someone else feels they have been wronged. This type of person probably reads and knows all the rules in the Employee Handbook.

This attitude can be caused by a person being closed-minded and therefore not understanding many things about their environment.

They often feel uncomfortable or confused about the world so they categorize and generalize. The writer Walt Whitman said, "Be curious, not judgmental" but these people are not able to do this. Specific types of judgmental attitudes in the workplace include: the inability to listen to a complaint from a customer or client with a clear head and without taking it personally; and the inability to see all points of view when considering what actions to take. It is possible that they will be negative rather than positive on the job and will look for others to recruit into their circle of closed-mindedness.

Vindictive

A strong sense of vindictiveness can also be a problem at work and in any type of organization. Those who score high on vindictiveness keep track of what they feel others owe them, remember slights for a long time, often complain about things, and are not afraid to confront and take action.

I remember the old song, "I shot the Sheriff, got ninety-nine years, and it sure has been a lesson to me." The problem is, I don't think vindictive people feel much regret. What is it with this mind-set? Vindictive people seem to feel compelled to "get even." This suggests that they see life as a zero-sum game where some people win and others have to lose. This is in contrast to most people who see the world in terms of cooperation where win-win possibilities dominate.

Vindictive people are quite proud of their assumptions. During my research, they made these statements: "If someone insults me, I remember it for a very long time;" "Don't get mad, get even;" and "I'm the wrong person to cross." Vindictive people tend to be mad most of the time.

Adversarial

This attitude can be a problem for any type of work environment and problems can arise from those who score high on adversarial. They get satisfaction from hurting others in small or large ways or by making others feel uncomfortable, they do not easily give respect or help, and if there is a request to change something they likely refuse even for the most mundane things.

Some types of work encourage a certain amount of adversarial attitudes such as the legal system, journalism, politics, and sports. The problem is when it becomes extreme and people lie or cheat to achieve the ends they want.

Some work environments have unions and management that are constantly fighting. The mood at work then becomes tense and adversarial all of the time. An additional issue with this type of stress is the physical toll it can take on everyone involved and, as a result of this, you often see good people leaving for other jobs.

Egocentric

This attitude can be a problem for any type of work environment and problems can arise from those who score high on egocentric. They always come first and the needs of the organization or those they work with always come last. Clients or customers can wait, new employees can figure things out on their own, teamwork is not their thing, and they cannot be depended on to work a little late or to adjust their schedule if there is a crisis.

Specific types of egocentric attitudes in the workplace include chronic talkers (those who talk at length about themselves so others cannot do their work), those who blame other workers for their own failures, and supervisors who expect the employees under them to do special/awkward favors, etc.

Occasionally, people with power can abuse their position because they are egocentric and feel that they are at the center of the universe. They can take advantage of those who work for them, i.e. those with no power, and if it is allowed to continue it can have dire consequences. Hubris has brought down many people in power.

Entitled

A strong sense of entitlement can make a person very difficult to work with in any type of organization. We know from the test that problems arise because the highly entitled assume that they are not being sufficiently rewarded, they tend to see work as an obligation rather than an opportunity, and they often feel put upon if they are asked to do anything extra.

Their expectations can be out of line with their skills and experience. They may demand a title they do not deserve, more money than is reasonable, and perks not yet earned.

Entitlement is an interesting attitude and it has, on occasion, been a source of humor. I am reminded of Woody Allen's lament, "Oh Lord if you could only give me a sign - - like putting 10 million dollars in a Swiss bank account in my name." Or the story of a man named Joseph who prayed every day for thirty years to win the lottery. One day on a hilltop he beseeched God and said "God, why have you not honored my prayer? I attend church every week, I tithe, I am good to my family and my fellow man and yet you don't honor my prayer." And God spoke to Joseph, "So Joseph, buy a ticket!"

Why do we find this so funny? I think it is because we all feel entitled to some degree but like the other attitudes measured in the test, those that are *extreme* cause problems.

Recently there has been a lot of buzz about generational differences concerning entitlement. Some argue that when you raise children where everyone gets a trophy, you are fostering entitlement. A recent generation has even been labeled the "Me Generation." Different generations may emphasize different attitudes but I caution you that attitudes or values are individual characteristics. This is where skilled interviewing and a good pre-employment test will help.

Insubordinate

This attitude also represents a problem for any type of work environment and problems can arise from those who score high on insubordinate. They attribute the success of others to luck rather than to their being qualified and deserving, feel that the chain of command can sometimes be disregarded, may not respect ranks, and if they don't understand instructions they may take action themselves.

Specific types of insubordination include refusal to carry out a clear order, abusive language, and lack of respect for other employees, customers, and supervisors. It can also include not showing up for work when there is no excuse or phone call, or showing up late every day. It is not easy to deal with these people and they may continue their ways even after warnings from supervisors. After a warning, they may decide to continue insubordination in quieter ways such as not making an important change in record keeping that was requested.

These people may have a chip on their shoulder or may have extreme disdain for authority. Supervisors should be trained in this area so they know the organization's specific definitions of insubordination and the appropriate actions to take.

Undisciplined

This attitude can be a problem for some organizations, but not all organizations -- as described at the beginning of this chapter. Those who score high on undisciplined have trouble concentrating, finishing a task, and setting priorities. They may have a history of this, starting when they were in school. When these people are made part of a team in the work environment they may do less work than expected because they figure other people on the team will do it.

There are simple ways we are disciplined such as punctuality, dressing appropriately for the job, and being polite. Then there are more critical ways such as staying motivated and understanding priorities. The bottom line for any organization is to be productive but with employees who are highly undisciplined it is very difficult for the organization to stay on track.

Some organizations should be especially watchful for those who score high on undisciplined. These include organizations that work with the elderly or with children, with the handicapped, or with those who are ill. These can be hospitals, nursing homes, rehab facilities, recreational facilities, childcare providers, etc. The highly undisciplined person may not be respectful of the special needs of others and may forget very important things. This year the news in the Washington, DC area included a story about a bus driver who left two young children with special needs at a place far away from their home; and another driver who forgot about two handicapped men in his car while he went shopping and to dinner. Fortunately the men were ok, and the two children, but this resulted in a court case which is something you never want.

Risk-inclined

This attitude can be a problem for some organizations, but not all organizations -- as described at the beginning of this chapter. Those who score high on risk-inclined do not take the time to fully understand a problem or refer to guidelines. When faced with a risky and challenging situation they feel that delays are expensive and should be avoided -- even if it may be good to delay a decision to get more information. If they are not sure how to proceed with a project, they may go full steam ahead on their own.

Risk in the workplace can be defined as the ability to understand uncertainty and its possible consequences. Some people actually hold the job title of Risk Officer and they weigh the pros and cons of various actions. The problem arises when a person is extremely risk-inclined and stops weighing the pros and cons. They can endanger themselves and others and they may do this for a variety of reasons such as thrill-seeking, greediness, laziness, or arrogance.

When the heads of Wall Street firms testified on Capitol Hill about the catastrophic events that started in 2008 some said they took the risks because everyone was doing it. They knew their investments were risky but felt if they did not offer them, clients would go elsewhere. When the BP oil-leak catastrophe happened in the Gulf of Mexico in 2010, some workers said they warned the company about safety problems a couple of weeks before the event but were ignored.

Fortunately, in most work environments, catastrophes are not looming and critical decisions are not required on a daily basis. A few organizations may look for those who take risks -- but they probably do not want it combined with arrogance.

Non-traditional

This is another attitude that can be a problem for some organizations, but not all organizations -- as described at the beginning of this chapter. Those who score high on non-traditional are focused on the future and have less respect for understanding past events. In the workplace they are not concerned with ceremonies and tradition, the organization's history, or even the rules and regulations.

Tradition serves a purpose in work environments and societies as a whole and a reasonable goal might be to find a balance between tradition and change. Some organizations are more open to change and try things such as job-sharing, telecommuting, and flexible hours. The federal government tries to be a model employer and often is the leader when it comes to new ways of doing things such as telecommuting. Many school systems are trying new ways of doing things such as charter schools, pay for performance, year-round schools, and a later starting time in the morning.

It is important to know if a job applicant is more comfortable in a formal or informal work environment. And how much of the non-traditional does your organization desire? If you want to shake things up, you may want a person who brings new ideas to the table. If you are happy with the organization as it is, then you want a more traditional person who will respect the rules and rituals that are in place.

Now that we have looked at the nine attitudes, it is important to remember our original objective - - we are looking for *extremes*. In short, strongly-held negative values lead to confrontation and problems and it is possible to be a jerk in a variety of ways.

Next we will look at the Workplace Attitudes Test instrument.

The Workplace Attitudes Test™

After identifying the nine attitudes that can lead to problems, I developed the Workplace Attitudes Test (WAT) which is a pre-employment test that measures the nine attitudes and identifies possible warning signals. WAT is a unique approach in the hiring process because it looks for the bad, not the good. As previously stated, it is like baking an upside-down cake.

What You Should Know About WAT

* WAT is also unique because I use an empirical approach to understanding jerks. In other words, I quantify it. When a job applicant takes the test, I use numbers to measure each of the nine attitudes and I also do an overall measurement. A high score on any of the nine attitudes or the overall measurement is a warning signal. This provides the job interviewer with a tool that is clear and easy to understand.

* WAT has been in the field for many years and is used by organizations in the U.S. and abroad. They include police academies, associations, government agencies, businesses, health systems, and colleges. My newest client uses WAT to help evaluate applicants who will work on oil rigs in Canada.

* WAT was developed for low- and mid-level workers rather than executives.

* WAT should be used as another tool in the hiring process and not the only tool.

* WAT understands that one shoe does not fit all. Different organizations may want strength in certain areas and not in others. For example, an organization with strict hierarchy such as the military or a large bank may desire a different mix of attitudes than an organization that is informal and has little hierarchy.

How WAT is Administered

WAT includes 45 forced-choice questions and takes most applicants about 15 minutes to complete. They can take the test on the Internet, by e-mail attachment, or by paper.

The results are summarized in a bar chart that shows the measurement of each of the nine attitudes as well as an overall score. High scores indicate possible warning signals. For example, a high score on judgmental means it is likely that this person has a propensity to intervene in controversies. A low or moderate score means they are likely not to do this, i.e. you probably want as many low or moderate scores as possible when hiring a new employee.

Remember that the workplace is an environment where positive attitudes are crucial. A person's attitudes are predictive of good or poor customer relations and disruptive or harmonious workplace behavior. The measurement of attitudes helps you see over the horizon and view potential problems which is always preferable to working in the dark or a murky haze.

The test has five questions for each of the nine attitudes. More specifically, it asks the applicant to complete sentences. Some examples follow and please note that the nine attitudes are shown here for demonstration purposes only, and they are *not* shown on the actual test.

The applicant is told that the test is self-explanatory. At the beginning it asks them to please complete each sentence by choosing A, B, or C so the sentence is most true from their perspective.

Sample WAT Questions

The job applicant completes each sentence by selecting one answer from A, B, or C that is most true from their perspective.

Note that the names of the attitudes in parentheses are *not* shown on the actual test.

(Judgmental)

Q Concerning my rights as an individual . . .

A. I feel that if I do not defend myself, no one else will.
B. on some occasions I feel it is necessary to defend myself.
C. basically, I am not very defensive so this is not much of an issue for me.

(Vindictive)

Q When someone insults or slights me . . .

A. I tend to remember it a very long time.
B. I can hold a grudge, but not often.
C. at first I get irritated, but soon forget it.

(Adversarial)

Q When someone tries to do something for me and fails, such as mispronouncing my name . . .

A. I often try to comfort that person and I may congratulate them for trying.
B. I reluctantly correct them if it will cause further embarrassment.
C. I tend to correct them because it is important that things be done right.

(Egocentric)

Q When my projects are completed . . .

A. I am more than willing to help a fellow worker with their projects.
B. once in a while I will pitch in.
C. I feel that I have earned the time to take a break and others have the same right.

(Entitled)

Q Concerning work . . .

A. having to work is one of life's necessities.
B. I do what is expected of me.
C. when working, I have often felt fortunate to have a job.

(Undisciplined)

Q When I have several tasks to do . . .

A. I tend to finish one and then go on to the next.
B. I tend to finish one project but I can still be flexible.
C. I sometimes jump around just to make things more
   interesting.

(Insubordinate)

Q Most people in positions of authority . . .

A. earned the right to be where they are.
B. are usually qualified and deserving.
C. often have been lucky and in the right place at the right
   time.

(Risk-Inclined)

Q When faced with a risky and challenging situation . . .

A. it is often good to delay a decision in order to get more
   information.
B. some delay is acceptable.
C. delays are often costly and should be avoided.

(Non-Traditional)

Q When in a new situation . . .

A. it is important to understand past events related to that situation.
B. the past is sometimes relevant.
C. the past is never as important as the future.

Each choice -- A, B, or C -- represents an answer that is considered low, moderate, or high. Low indicates a person who likely gets along well in the workplace, and high indicates a person who may have problems. (Note that the low, moderate, and high answers are not listed in the same order for every question.)

There is a group of five questions for each attitude. To get a warning signal for a specific attitude, a person has to answer three questions as high and at least two questions as moderate in that group. I designed the system so that it is *not* easy to get a warning signal for a specific attitude.

I also do an overall score based on the three highest attitude scores.

How to Order WAT

Go to the web site at www.WorkplaceAttitudes.com for more information and to order the test. Or send an e-mail to AllegianceResearch@gmail.com.

Reporting WAT Results

One page says it all. WAT reports the results from each test in a bar chart. In fact, one number provides most of the information you need -- the cumulative warning signal should not be 70 or above (note the horizontal line which is 70 in the chart).

The Workplace Attitudes Test™
How Likely is This Person to be Disruptive?

The Cumulative Warning Signal for this person is 37

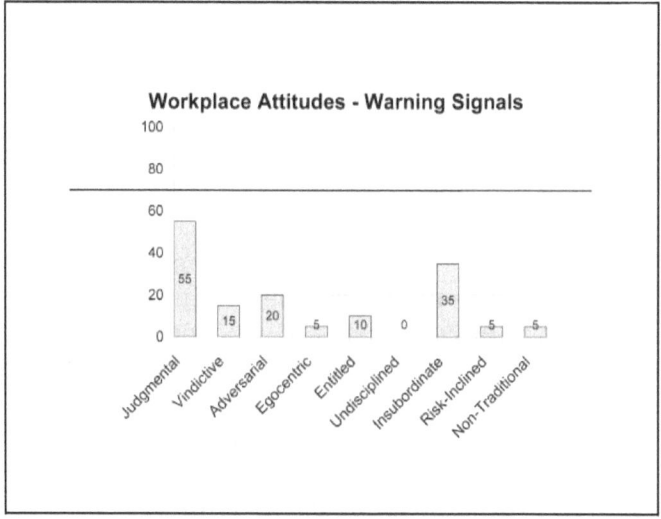

Judgmental	55
Vindictive	15
Adversarial	20
Egocentric	5
Entitled	10
Undisciplined	0
Insubordinate	35
Risk-Inclined	5
Non-Traditional	5

Interpreting WAT Results

Attending to these results will make you a better interviewer. Remember that people are often hired for their aptitudes and fired for their attitudes. If you pay careful attention to warning signals, you are unlikely to make a mistake in hiring because of qualifications and not considering attitudes. Here is the scoring key.

Low	0 to 29
Moderate	30 to 69
High	70 to 100

The bar chart shows nine attitudes related to disruption in the workplace and **scores of 70 or above may indicate potential problems**. My research suggests that these attitudes help determine behavior toward customers, clients, fellow workers, supervisors, and work in general. I also calculate a cumulative warning score that is based on a formula using the top three scores. As with the score for each attitude, a cumulative score of 70 or above may be of concern.

High warning signals suggest a propensity for confrontation meaning that the respondent may have difficulty getting along with others in the work environment. Low or moderate warning signals suggest the opposite and the respondent will likely be sensitive to the needs of others in a work environment.

If there is only one high warning signal, this should be discussed in greater detail with the applicant. If you are satisfied with the explanations, you may still want to work with this person.

When looking at work-related attitudes it is important to understand your own work environment. For example, a formal organization may desire an employee who is low on "risk-inclined" while an informal organization may desire an employee who is more "risk-inclined" if it is looking for entrepreneurial ideas.

It is possible for a person to have a high warning signal for one attitude and be low on the others. As an example, a person can be high on entitled and low on the other attitudes, i.e. this means that they can feel very entitled but will probably not be undisciplined or insubordinate.

Some organizations may prefer a certain combination of attitudes. For example, law enforcement may expect high "judgmental" but it should be coupled with moderate or low "egocentric." Remember that you are looking for a good match for your organization. Overall, pay careful attention to high warning-signals.

This test should be used in conjunction with good interviewing techniques and other good practices related to hiring and promoting.

In Summary: Why Does The Workplace Attitudes Test Work?

I think that WAT works for some very simple reasons: it has a limited objective; it is based on understanding attitudes from the right cohort; people are fairly open about their beliefs and values which form the basis for attitudes; and extreme or disruptive behavior results from holding certain attitudes in the extreme. Let's look at each point.

Limited Objective

When I set out to develop the WAT I sought to answer a simple question. Do disruptive workers share certain identifiable attitudes? I made the assumption that the workplace is almost always a social environment and I wanted to understand individuals who do not get along well with others. This is much easier than trying to understand personality or trying to match people to a certain type of job. Personality has many components and jobs can be done in a variety of ways, but there appears to be a limited number of ways to be disruptive in the workplace.

The Right Cohort

A cohort is simply a group of people who share some characteristic. Fortunately they're not hard to find and in this case they tend not to be bashful. I started with open-ended interviews of good and bad employees (former or current), and then I used the results to identify nine attitudes as leading to potential problems in the workplace. An instrument was developed to measure these attitudes and it was validated by testing over 300 people. The scores were correlated with their behavior to confirm my hypotheses. Persons with high WAT scores (warning signals) had more supervisor ratings indicating disruptive behavior, more job turnover in the past five years, and more dislike of work in general.

Beliefs and Values

Short of saying, "Yes I am a jerk," these people are quite willing to talk about their beliefs and values which are the underpinnings of their attitudes. Oftentimes they talk freely to amplify their low opinion of others. You've heard of the term "a people person," well these are "anti-people persons." Where Will Rogers said he never met a person he didn't like, these individuals almost never met people that they do like. It is like the pundit who said, "I love humanity, it is people I don't like."

Now to understand beliefs and values one must ask open-ended questions. This is much like the jury-consultant approach. They ask questions such as, "What do you think of the justice system?" And then, "Why do you think that?" or "Why do you feel that way?" Here is a glimpse of some of the answers and attitudes during my interviews.

"Most people are stupid." "You can't trust anybody." "My boss is so ignorant." "Work sucks but you have to do it." "I never get a break." "I should be making more money." And one of my favorites, "Step on my toes and forget to apologize and I'll kick your ass -- I don't care who you are." I was wise enough not to suggest steel-toed shoes for the last one. I could go on but you get the idea. Next let's look at some of the attitudes that underlie these sentiments.

Extreme Attitudes

The big nine attitudes that can potentially lead to disruption in the workplace are:
> Judgmental
> Vindictive
> Adversarial
> Egocentric
> Entitled
> Undisciplined
> Insubordinate
> Risk-Inclined
> Non-Traditional

I found a strong correlation between disruptive behavior and holding the above-mentioned attitudes in the extreme. In the WAT I developed a group of five questions for each of the nine attitudes. Each question has three possible answers -- one weak, one moderate and one extreme. The respondent chooses the one answer that is most true from their point of view. For example, here is a question and three possible answers for the judgmental attitude.

When I feel I have been treated unjustly . . .

* I will do whatever is necessary to defend my rights.
* I seldom feel I have been treated unfairly.
* I probably should do more but oftentimes just let it go.

In this case, the first answer is considered extreme. To get a warning signal for judgmental, this person has to answer three questions as extreme and at least two questions as moderate in that group. I designed the system so that it is *not* easy to get a warning signal for a specific attitude.

Respondents have strong rationales for their extreme answers and these extremes are strongly related to disruptive behavior. This test works because people tend to be proud of their attitudes and they use them to justify their behavior. Although job candidates may not reveal this information in a job interview, oftentimes because it is never asked, they are willing to express themselves in the test.

There you have it. The WAT works because it doesn't try to do too much, it is based on understanding the right people, they are willing to reveal their attitudes if given the right setting, and strongly-held bad attitudes are related to disruptive behavior in the workplace

It would seem to be quite difficult to achieve extreme scores but about one in twenty people do it. When they are interviewed concerning their answers, they tend to report that their answers accurately reflect their view of the world. This is, after all, what attitudes are defined to be. They are the filters through which we see the world. This reminds me of the Spanish expression "cada cabeza es un mundo." It translates to "each head is a world." Our goal is to understand those worlds so they don't collide. I'll have to admit that I might have carried this analogy too far but if you really want to use your "cabeza," pay attention to negative attitudes.

Evaluating Existing Employees

That sums up the primary purpose of the WAT. It is a pre-employment test but many companies have used it to evaluate and help existing employees. I used to think that this was a little like closing the barn door after the horses escaped. After all, once a person has worked for your organization you should know who has problem attitudes.

The test measures bad attitudes and these are difficult to discuss face-to-face with current employees. For example, an interviewer might not want to say "I see here that you are quite judgmental" or "I note that you tend to be vindictive." Dale Carnegie who wrote *How to Win Friends and Influence People* would not approve.

You can have the information but you don't need to state it in a negative way. Each attitude relevant to the workplace is not a single dimension, rather it exists on a continuum. That is, each bad attitude that is related to "disruptive behavior" has a corresponding attitude that is related to "getting along with people." This is demonstrated below with the nine attitudes.

Accepting versus Judgmental

Forgiving versus Vindictive

Accommodating versus Adversarial

People-Oriented versus Egocentric

Unassuming versus Entitled

Self-Disciplined versus Undisciplined

Respectful versus Insubordinate

Cautious versus Risk-Inclined

Traditional versus Non-Traditional

The research has shown that the bad attitudes are disruptive only when they are extreme. When working with existing employees and reporting the results, it may be better for the interviewer to emphasize the positive results rather than any negative results.

Improving the Work Environment

Although it is the primary goal of the Workplace Attitudes Test to screen out potentially disruptive employees it can also be useful for matching people to different types of workplace environments and to help some employees perform their jobs better.

In terms of matching people to work environments, command-and-control workplaces will likely find that individuals with respect for tradition and authority tend to fit in better. Conversely, entrepreneurial or team-building organizations may not need as much respect for authority and tradition and may prosper with people who are more self-disciplined and people-oriented.

The test can also help some employees perform their job better. In one example, WAT helped a young supervisor work with older sales reps. Joyce was in her late twenties and supervised six sales reps who were twice her age. She did a great job. All of her reports were done on time even if she had to work overtime, all of her staff liked her, business was good, but she was miserable.

She wasn't sure why she was miserable and discussions with her boss didn't help much. The big boss wanted to keep her and gave her raises and more time off, but still she was miserable. At that time, WAT was under development and the entire staff agreed to take it. In the results, no one had high warning signals but the test solved the mystery.

Joyce proved to be accepting, forgiving, accommodating, people-oriented, unassuming, self-disciplined, respectful of authority, somewhat cautious, and very traditional. Her scores on the test were low for all the attitudes. (A low score indicates a person who is likely to get along well in the workplace.)

Joyce's sales reps were, well, sales reps. They had some good people skills but respect for authority, self-discipline, and entitlement were somewhat of an issue. They scored moderately in these three areas.

In short, Joyce wanted to please people, and her sales reps tended to take advantage of her. She met everyone's needs but her own. The sales reps sometimes were slow in meeting deadlines for their reports, talked to her at length without respect for her time, and tended to feel they were special.

I am reminded of a great quote from the movie, *Three Days of the Condor,* when a young CIA agent during the Cold War asks a grizzled old veteran played by John Houseman, "What do you miss about the old days (referring to World War II)?" Houseman replied, "The clarity."

Joyce finally had clarity and the story has a happy ending. Joyce got a private office and a gatekeeper secretary. The sales reps could no longer barge in and talk to her socially at anytime. They had to make an appointment unless it was critical. Joyce also decided to give them an incentive to get their reports in on time.

Joyce regained her sanity and the organization kept a good supervisor.

Are Ya Feeling Lucky Punk, Well Are Ya?

These immortal words were uttered in the *Dirty Harry* movie played by a gun-wielding Clint Eastwood whose gun may or may not have been out of ammunition. Eastwood also uttered the words "Make my day!" in a similar situation. Such is the work of cinematic policemen administering quick and final justice.

Truth be told, some police spend their entire careers without firing their guns outside of the firing range. Most like it that way. Police work is difficult and oftentimes dangerous. They go where there are problems and they often see the seamier side of life. It is a challenging career and I am happy to say that WAT has been utilized to help screen people for police work.

In most professions one does not want a person who is judgmental, vindictive, adversarial and egocentric. But when looking at work-related attitudes, it is important to understand your own work environment and some organizations may prefer a certain combination of attitudes. For example, law enforcement may want high judgmental which is defined as a strong sense of right and wrong yet it should be coupled with moderate or low egocentric. We want police to enforce rules and regulations. That is their job. We also want police who have people skills, a sense of forgiveness, and the ability for accommodation.

This is expecting a lot, but thousands of law enforcement people do just that every day.

Conclusion

Look, we've talked about a lot of things including how to cope with workplace jerks and here's the bottom line.

* You need to eliminate disruptive employees in your workplace and you need to identify potential employees with the attitudes that you don't want.

* Unfortunately, the job interview does not do a good job at identifying bad attitudes because people will say what they think you want to hear.

* Other pre-employment tests concentrate on desirable characteristics.

My solution works because it is like an upside down cake -- its only purpose is to identify potential employees with bad attitudes. If you test for good workplace attitudes, you will always find some good attitudes. Everyone has some good attitudes but not everyone has bad attitudes.

Look for what you *don't* want, the bad attitudes, otherwise you will miss them. As I mentioned at the beginning of this book one of my clients said, "We hire good employees by not hiring bad ones."

Think of the WAT as an insurance policy. It's a little like the Fram Oil Filter Ad—"Pay me now or pay me later." It is like an insurance policy but it is also more than that. You buy insurance because you want to be compensated when something bad happens; you buy the WAT to *prevent* something bad from happening.

Our statistics show that about one in twenty hires is a bad one. That's about five percent. George Carlin observed, "Have you ever wondered why everyone who drives faster than you is a maniac, and everyone who drives slower than you is an idiot?" Some days it may seem to you that everyone is a big jerk but according to my research it really is about five percent.

Yes, about one in twenty potential employees has an attitude problem. How many times have you had thoughts like this, "I have never killed a man, but I have read many obituaries with great pleasure." This was a quote from Clarence Darrow. Or along the same line, consider this quote from Mark Twain, "I didn't attend the funeral, but I sent a nice letter saying I approved of it."

Now, at least in the workplace, you don't have to have these sentiments. You can screen out these people before nature does it for you.

Appendix A

If You Bought This Book You Can Enter Our Contest

Yes, you can really win a chocolate turkey covered in foil. You can eat it right away, display until it goes stale, or freeze it and forget about it. The turkey will be sent to you by FedEx, UPS, or the US Post Office, whichever is the most turkey-friendly. You can even pose with your new little friend and I will post the picture on my web site

We're looking for a great story based on your experiences with jerks. Here are the categories.

- Most insulting to customers

- Most costly in terms of dollars and cents

- Most difficult to supervise

- Biggest PR disaster

- Worst lawsuit

- and . . . I can't believe this jerk.

Now, the rules. To protect the guilty, I don't want the real name of your company or the employee. You may refer to the person by a creative nickname or initials. For the company you probably should not use something like Starbutts or MicroFluff. For the employee, schmuck, schlemiel, jerk, or turkey would be all right. Just send in a brief description, maybe a few paragraphs, of their behavior on the job. This doesn't need to be of the scope of Enron or BP. I want ordinary rude and boorish behavior. You know, self-centered idiocy that makes us want to strangle someone. Send to AllegianceResearch@gmail.com.

Appendix B

An Interview with Dale Paulson

Q What is the Workplace Attitudes Test (WAT)?

A It is a pre-employment test that measures work-related attitudes and it takes most people about fifteen minutes to complete. The attitudes measured help predict workplace behavior and how likely a person is to be disruptive. There is more information at our web site, www.WorkplaceAttitudes.com.

Q Why is it so important?

A Ninety percent of your problems usually come from a very small percent of your employees.

Q Why does WAT work when other tests and job interviews don't?

A We turned the test development process on its head. Rather than investigate good employees to see why they are good, we looked at problem employees to determine why they are bad. We found nine attitudes that predict problem behavior in the workplace.

Q What is the best way to demonstrate how WAT is really different from other pre-employment tests?

A I like to take the humorous approach: We can help you hire someone who is insubordinate, adversarial, egocentric and undisciplined. I can practically guarantee that they will alienate fellow workers and drive away customers. Of course, we can do the opposite too . . . we can help you avoid hiring people with bad attitudes.

Q How common are "bad attitudes" in the workplace?

A Our research has found about one in twenty employees has bad attitudes. Unfortunately, the job interview doesn't do a very good job of identifying these people. Everyone is polite in a job interview and questions about attitude are not usually asked.

Q How are the results presented?

A The nine workplace attitudes are presented on a bar chart and each attitude is measured with a vertical bar. There is also a cumulative warning signal. Based on my research, scores of 70 or above are considered warning signals. You also receive an instruction sheet for interpreting the results. A sample of the results is in the earlier Chapter entitled "Reporting WAT Results."

Q Who can benefit from using this test?

A The test has been designed for entry-level and mid-level people but it has also been very effective for selecting supervisors. If you are concerned about how your customers, clients, or co-workers are treated, this is the test for you. It has been used by businesses, police, associations, government agencies, etc.

Q How does a person order the test?

A You can order the test at www.WorkplaceAttitudes.com and pay through PayPal. Then PayPal notifies us of your order and we send you the web site address where your job applicant can take the test. We usually send you the results the same day. You can also contact us directly by e-mail at AllegianceResearch@gmail.com for the information.

Appendix C

We Say, You Say

If you buy the Workplace Attitudes Test (WAT) here is what we say to you.

Congratulations:

You are about to enter a new era of employee selection. This is truly a breakthrough. Now for the first time you can understand the values and attitudes that motivate potential employees. When selecting new hires you can avoid the landmines while you pick the cherries.

Without getting too complicated, we analyze workplace attitudes to predict likely behavior.

Wouldn't you like to avoid potential employees who may sue you or your company? How about identifying possible gadflies who would rather socialize than work? Maybe you would like to know about people who are likely to be hostile to your customers or clients?

Conversely, how would you like to find people who are likely to be grateful to have a job, who are willing to put in extra effort, and who are team players?

Now you can.

All you need to do is have the job candidate take the WAT which consists of forty-five questions and we will evaluate it for you. You then receive a bar chart that measures the individual's relevant workplace attitudes in nine areas and an overall score that tells you how likely they are to be disruptive in the workplace. Remember, everyone is on their best behavior during the job interview. With WAT you are in a position to hire good employees by avoiding bad ones. It makes you a better interviewer and applies to a variety of environments including business, non-profits, and the public sector.

Here are some comments by users of the WAT.

"This (the WAT) is not a psychological test, it simply tells you if the person you are considering can get along with others. You need this information."
Association Executive

"If you could send your candidate to boot camp like the military, you wouldn't need this test. But then again, maybe you would because some recruits wash out."
Retired Army Sergeant

"We wanted someone who would enforce the rules and yet would get along with people. This mix is important in our business and the WAT helped us find the right person."
Marina Manager

"You can't believe the number of jerks out there. I interview a lot of kids for summer jobs and some are pampered and spoiled. The WAT screener makes my job much easier. At an amusement park you want patient and polite employees. Believe me, this separates the wheat from shaft."
Amusement Park Manager

"With a money back guarantee, it's a no-brainer."
Fast Food Franchise Owner

"By keeping it simple and concentrating on bad attitudes, this thing really works."
Police Academy Superintendent

"In my opinion, HR is so focused on keeping people out that they keep a lot of good people from getting the job. The WAT keeps bad-attitude people from getting the job."
Department Store Manager

"If you don't want to ask someone 'Are you an asshole?' you should use this test."
Locksmith Store Owner

"Some people are proud to be jerks and others hide it during the interview. Now you can catch them in the act."
Motorcycle Store Owner

"Wow, this thing (the WAT) couldn't be easier, one score and a bar graph. No warning signals, no problem."
Health System VP

"One less thing to worry about. We like the quick turnaround for the results and always appreciate this valuable information. This is why we are a long-time WAT user."
Local Government Executive

"$29 bucks, you're kidding me? (I mean this in a good way.)"
Supervisor, Boat Supply Store

"I haven't tried other tests and probably won't. This works. Thanks."
Tour Company Director

"If you think that this test is better than just an interview, you're a better interviewer than me."
Restaurant Manager

"Believe me, there are bad apples out there and this test keeps them out of your barrel."
Auto Shop Owner

"I used the WAT on about ten new hires and there were no problems. Then I got a little lax and decided I didn't need it. I hired the next group of people without it and one of them resulted in a sexual harassment suit that was settled out of court. As a result, I am back to using the WAT."
Lawn Service and Nursery Manager

"We promoted a clean-freak perfectionist for our fabric and sewing store, thinking that this was a good thing. There are no fabric remnants on the floor but some of our best sales clerks have quit and customer complaints are rampant. From now on I'll be using the Workplace Attitudes test for promoting supervisors as well as new hires."
Sewing and Fabric Store Chain

Our clients use WAT to screen for potentially disruptive employees. These clients are happy they did not hire these people and who knows how many problems they avoided? Some clients also like to use WAT to test employees before promoting them to supervisors and they probably have also avoided potential problems. And some use it to match people to different types of organizations such as team-building organizations and hierarchical organizations

Appendix D

Workplace Attitudes Test™ Fact Sheet

Remember, just because Ben Franklin wanted to make the turkey our national bird doesn't mean you have to hire one!

The workplace is an environment where positive attitudes are crucial. A person's attitudes are predictive of good or poor customer relations and disruptive or harmonious workplace behavior. But how do you *measure* attitudes? The WAT is a pre-employment test that enables employers to look at nine attitudes relevant to the workplace and identify possible warning signals. It includes 45 questions, takes about 15 minutes, and results are summarized in a bar chart. Here is a list of the nine attitudes with those that can lead to problems in bold.

Nine Attitudes Relevant to the Workplace

Judgmental versus accepting
Propensity to defend one's rights, a strong sense of right and wrong, may have the compulsion to intervene in a controversy.

Vindictive versus forgiving
Tends to keep track of obligations as well as perceived slights and insults, may persist in attempts to "correct" the situation.

Adversarial versus accommodating
Limited understanding of the needs and desires of other people and generally-accepted social obligations. May get satisfaction from confronting or hurting others.

Egocentric versus people oriented
May be disinclined to assist fellow workers, limited obligation to customers, and a general unwillingness to make sacrifices for the good of the organization.

Entitled versus unassuming
May assume that they are not being rewarded sufficiently, tends to see work as an obligation rather than an opportunity, and may have a sense of entitlement.

Undisciplined versus self-disciplined
Limited commitment to finish projects without supervision, has trouble concentrating and setting priorities, may not pull their weight as a team member.

Insubordinate versus respectful
Tends to doubt people in authority and the chain of command, may question that "rank has its privileges," oftentimes unwilling to seek help from a superior.

Risk-Inclined versus cautious
Generally unwilling to delay decisions in order to get more information, disinclined to check with others, and limited regard for record keeping.

Non-Traditional versus traditional
Oftentimes little desire to understand past events, rules and regulations, or work-related ceremonies.

How to Order the Test

Go to the web site at www.WorkplaceAttitudes.com for more information and to order the test. Or send an e-mail to AllegianceResearch@gmail.com.

This Fact Sheet May be Duplicated

This two-page Fact Sheet can be duplicated so you can share the information as long as it is not changed and Dr. Dale Paulson is credited.

Appendix E

We Offer a 100% Money-Back Guarantee and Frankly it Isn't Worth a Tinker's Dam

If you're wondering what a tinker's dam is, it is usually defined as something that is worthless. Some think that it was a curse as in a tinker's damn which was considered of little significance because tinkers were always swearing; or that it is a tinker's dam which is a small dam to hold solder made by tinkers when mending pans and after being used is of no value. See the following web site for definitions, www.phrases.org.uk/meanings/tinkers-damn.html.

I lean towards the second tinker's dam definition. Albeit, why would I say that the guarantee for the Workplace Attitudes Test (WAT) is worthless? The WAT is designed to ensure that you don't hire a person with a bad attitude in the workplace. Presumably, if you are asking for your money back you have hired a "turkey." This puts you in a bit of a sticky wicket which is defined as a difficult situation.

(A wicket is the playing surface used in cricket. It is a direct allusion to the difficulty of playing on a wet and sticky pitch. www.phrases.org.uk/meanings/334550.html)

Overall, you've hired the wrong person and a few dollars back from us isn't going to help you much. Fortunately, the Workplace Attitudes Test works well and no one has ever asked for their money back.

About the Author

Dale Paulson, Ph.D., is President of Allegiance Research Group where he enjoys developing innovative research products and quantifying human behavior. He has done research for over 100 national organizations and has received several trademarks for his methodologies. His Workplace Attitudes Test™ has been on the market for over ten years and is the subject of this book.

He is also a speaker, a frequent writer of articles, and a guest on radio programs. For those interested in reading more about his research, take a look at his chapter on using pictographs in the book, *Brick & Mortar Shopping in the 21st Century*; or read his book entitled *Allegiance: Fulfilling the Promise of One-to-One Marketing for Associations* that describes nine types of members.

He is a native of Minnesota and lives with his wife in the Washington, DC area.